1776

1778

1785

1787

MOUNT VERNON

THE LIBRARY
AT MOUNT VERNON

By
Frances Laverne Carroll
and
Mary Meacham

Beta Phi Mu 1977

Beta Phi Mu Chapbook Number Twelve
Published by Beta Phi Mu, Pittsburgh, Pennsylvania
Copyright © Frances Laverne Carroll and Mary Meacham, 1977

Library of Congress Cataloging in Publication Data

Carroll, Frances Laverne, 1925-
   The library at Mount Vernon.

   (Beta Phi Mu chapbook; no. 12)
   Bibliography: p.
   Includes index.
   1. Washington, George, Pres. U.S., 1732-1799 — Library. 2. Mount
Vernon. I. Meacham, Mary, 1946-   joint author. II. Title. III. Series:
Beta Phi Mu. Chapbook   ; no. 12.
Z997.W32C36   027'.1'755291   77-22482
ISBN 0-910230-12-9

Foreword

For the twelfth of its series, Beta Phi Mu is publishing a chapbook by two of its female members. Why the chapbooks have been so long dominated by male authors is a mystery, perhaps unpardonable, perhaps explainable because so few manuscripts have been submitted by female writers. In recent months female authors have submitted an increasing number of manuscripts, several of which came very near acceptance, and the Publishing Committee is hopeful that the trend will continue and that the balance between the sexes will soon be adjusted.

Although *The Library at Mount Vernon* was submitted during the bicentennial year, its acceptance for publication was purely coincidental. While its publication proves that Beta Phi Mu is not unmindful of the period through which we are passing, the criterion for selection was that it be a significant contribution to the literature of books and libraries.

The authors of this chapbook are both on the faculty of the School of Library Science, University of Oklahoma. Frances Laverne Carroll is a professor of Library Science, specializing in school libraries, is author of several articles on international library education and school libraries, and is national series editor for the American Library Association's annotated bibliographies, *Reading for Young People*. Mary Meacham is an instructor in Library Science, specializing in children's literature, and is author of a recent article on school libraries in *International Library Review*.

Designer for the chapbook is Bill Williams, director of publications at the University of Oklahoma. Several of his publications have won awards for excellence of design. He is currently serving as president of the University and College Designers Association.

D.B.

Frances Laverne Carroll

Mary Meacham

Bill Williams.

v

Preface

The description of the library of George Washington at Mount Vernon is for those who are interested in a library in the traditional sense. Many today may wish for the space and the freedom to enjoy the space that a private home library provides. A few would see the formality and order exemplified at Mount Vernon as the rigid design of early architecture. For the majority, however, there is an appreciation for the preservation of Mount Vernon by the Mount Vernon Ladies' Association of the Union. The research of the book could not have been accomplished without its assistance. A deep respect for the work of restoration has been generated during the time devoted to the writing of this manuscript. Several members of the staff of Mount Vernon have been exceptionally helpful in assisting with the research. Particularly useful have been the **Annual reports** of the Association and the **Notebooks**, which have not been included in the bibliography, and the illustration file in the Research Library at Mount Vernon.

Probably more than any other person of his time George Washington represents through his private library collection the feeling that any person has at the present time for books and a home library. His collection was not exemplary and his library room was not exceedingly well-planned, but his attempt to meet his needs with his resources was a true expression of his individuality.

A million visitors each year on an average see Mount Vernon, and the last major room they see on touring the mansion is the library. Washington's conception of the acquirement of knowledge is expressed in that room and is stated: *"I conceive a knowledge of books is the basis upon which other knowledge is to be built."* This book is dedicated to enlarging the understanding of the irreplacable — knowledge as exemplified by libraries.

The authors wish to express their special thanks to W. David Zittell, John A. Castellani, and Ellen McCallister for their help and encouragement in the preparation of this work.

F. L. Carroll
Mary Meacham

Spring, 1976

Acknowledgements for photographs and drawings:
   The Mount Vernon Ladies' Association
   The Boston Athenaeum
   Taylor Lewis and Associates
   Mario Tur

Table of Contents

LIST OF ILLUSTRATIONS

Frontispeice

Chapter I

1. **Young Man's Companion**

Chapter II

1. Story-and-a-half Cottage
2. View of the Potomac River
3. Five Farms
4. The Plan for Unity of Buildings
5. Pantry and Reconstructed Closet
6. Dressing Table
7. Detail Drawings

Chapter III

1. Breakfast Table
2. Breakfront Secretary-Bookcase
3. Watermark
4. Copying Press

Chapter IV

LIST OF COLOR PLATES

THE LIBRARY
AT
MOUNT VERNON

CHAPTER I

Colonial Libraries and the Young Washington

Before the Pilgrims arrived in America in the late 1500's, a "very tolerable" library in England was one of at least three hundred volumes. Not everyone could afford this, of course; many people, such as country gentlemen, curates, and vicars, had one to two hundred volumes.[1] These consisted largely of theological works (including Bibles and prayer books), stories of chivalry, songs, joke books, some classical works, politics and history, and the ever-popular handbooks or "how to" books, as they are often called today, very popular disquisitions telling one how to do all sorts of useful things, such as farming and carpentry.

There were no American literary masterpieces during the first hundred and fifty years after the Pilgrims arrived. Not until the early 1700's when George Washington was a young man were there any literary creations of importance in America. Between 1607 and the early 1700's, the few American writers of lasting works included the historians and religious writers William Bradford, John Winthrop, the Mathers, Robert Beverly, and Jonathan Edwards, and more general writers such as Benjamin Franklin and Roger Williams. There were also a few noteworthy American poets such as Anne Bradstreet and Edward Taylor.

During George Washington's boyhood, therefore, the American books to which he might have been exposed were few in number. Of the American books of this period, there were only two itemized in the inventory of his library — Beverly's *History of Virginia* and *The Works of John Winthrop*.[2]

When the early settlers came to America, they often brought along their books (as well as memories of having attended Oxford or Cambridge and a habit of reading),[3] and the shipments of books ordered from England soon enriched these early collections further. True American literature was:

> somewhat meager in volume and undistinguished in quality. It is quite understandable that a people clinging to a foothold on the edge of a vast mysterious continent, constantly assailed on their western frontier by a savage and implacable foe whom they were trying to despoil of his lands, would have little time for literary diversions, particularly so-called belles lettres.[4]

It was not unusual, however, for early colonial libraries to have several hundred volumes. In Plymouth, in the 1630's, small private libraries, mostly devotional in nature, were common. William Brewster, for example, had about four hundred volumes when he died in 1643; Miles Standish and William Bradford had a more modest fifty and eighty books, respectively. John Winthrop, Jr., governor of Connecticut, had accumulated over one thousand volumes by 1640; other early settlers, Samual Eaton of New Haven, Connecticut, and John Goodburne in Virginia, had libraries which had been brought from Europe.[5] There is even mention of a Puritan circulating library kept in Henry Smith's house on Beech Hill, Goose Creek. A Negro slave carried the books to members in a cowhide bag to protect them from the weather.[6] The first bookseller and publisher, Hezekiah Usher, opened his store in Cambridge in 1639.[7]

Most of the New England libraries, as we might expect, consisted largely of theology with little literature (although Brewster had a volume or two of poetry and history), little mathematics, or geography, and perhaps a few classical works. However, Wright feels that the early colonial libraries had less emphasis on theological and religious works than is sometimes believed.[8] Colonial books, on the whole, probably consisted of religious commentaries, translations of Latin and Greek works, a few histories of the colonies, school books, legal and medical handbooks, and such practical books as those that told the value of coins in the various colonies.[9] Cotton Mather began his library when he was nineteen, in 1682, with ninety-six volumes, eighty-one of which were theological and the rest historical, philosophical, and philological.[10] This library had eventually grown to nearly four thousand volumes when Mather died in 1728.

Governor Winthrop had the largest and most influential scientific library in America in the late 1600's. It consisted of over one thousand volumes, including religion, history, travel, philosophy, and law, as well as science. It was open to his friends and neighbors, and he gave thirty-nine books to Harvard. The Reverend Samuel Lee came from England with a large number of scientific books in 1686; this collection was offered for sale in 1693 by a Boston bookseller, its dissemination stimulating scientific interest in New England.[11]

There are early mentions of Virginia libraries, such as John Goodburne's in 1635. These had generally more of the Greek and Latin classics than in New England, but dogmatic religious books predominated here also. William Fitzhugh of Virginia in 1671 had a library of history, law, medicine, physics, and morals, but not literature, essays, poetry or romances. In the 1600's, except for the semi-public libraries and the booksellers, most collections of books were owned by clergymen, lawyers, doctors, well-to-do merchants, and planters.[12] The first three of these often had books outside their respective fields of interest. The minister's library was often the largest in a town in colonial times, and books were frequently lent from it. The first public library in the British colonies was established at a projected college at Heunco, Virginia; it flourished with bequests of books from English estates.[13]

These early Virginia libraries began to show a practical as well as purely literary content. A popular book published a few years later, for example, in 1734, was *Every Man his own Doctor, or the Poor Planter's Physician*, which Benjamin Franklin printed and sold.[14] As the title suggests, it was a guidebook for the home treatment of various diseases. It may be "easy to forget the quiddities of the library and drawing room in a forest,"[15] but in spite of the hardships of colonial life, the planters seem to have retained the essence of the library. In the late 1600's libraries became larger and more numerous in New England and Virginia. In the latter half of the seventeenth century the Byrd family's outstanding library at Westover was begun. Of the three generations of Byrds important in colonial history, the Honorable William Byrd II was the most influential. He had collected between thirty-six hundred and four thousand volumes when he died in 1744, and his library was one of the largest private libraries in America at that time.[16] Elsewhere in Virginia, Robert "King" Carter of Corotoman had an extensive library when he died in 1732, and his son Councilman Carter of Nomini Hall later had fifteen hundred volumes. Arthur Spicer in 1701 had a good collection of law books, a common practice because the planters so often had to act as their own lawyers, particularly in the tangled land claims which were common. The Lees and Wormeleys also had "considerable collections."[17]

Book printing began in America in 1640 when Stephen Daye set up a press in the basement of the house of Harvard's president and printed the famous *Whole Book of Psalms.* (This had been preceded by a broadsheet published by Daye the year before; many books *by* colonists had been published abroad also.) By the 1680's booksellers in Boston were doing a thriving business.[18] There was, however, a considerable importing of English and European books in the late 1600's and until at least the mid-1700's; Virginia continued to rely on foreign books for an even longer time, partly due to the suppression of printing by Governor Berkeley in 1682, who remarked that Virginia had neither free schools nor printing, and he hoped it would not have for three hundred years.[19] Franklin said that in 1722 there was not a good bookseller south of Boston, and this was true for Virginia although exaggerated in regard to the other colonies. Williamsburg, Virginia, did not have a bookstore until 1736.[20]

There were many private libraries all over the colonies by the early 1700's and several cities, Boston, New York, Philadelphia, and Charleston, had an extensive book business,[21] but Virginia, with no large leading city, continued to ·order from England. Much of English bookselling in the 1700's was to private libraries.[22] Many books from London did not pass through an American bookshop, and each planter had to decide for himself what to buy (often sight unseen) or let his factor (purchasing agent) do it for him.[23] In colonial America it was very fashionable for the great planters of the South to have a library although books were far from plentiful.[24] Some foreign visitors in the 1700's were impressed by how many French books the plantation libraries had.[25] The works of Addison, Steele, Pope, Congreve, and Prior were common in the great plantation houses and several planters were interested in botany.[26] Nonetheless, "in the training of a gentleman the emphasis was thoroughly practical. He was judged less by the furnishings of his mind, than by the furniture of his house. . . ."[27]

Individual borrowing from private libraries was common, at least among acquaintances. In addition to private home libraries there existed in some of the colonies, in the very late 1600's, semi-private libraries. Dr. Thomas Bray, later one of the founders of the Society for the Propagation of the Gospel in Foreign Parts, was sent to establish the Church of England in Maryland and to improve the lot of clergymen, who suffered from a scarcity of books. Bray founded parochial libraries in thirty parishes in Maryland, which, although intended primarily for the clergy, were free, circulating libraries, open to any resident. He also began libraries as far north as New York and as far south as Georgia, eventually numbering about one hundred. The libraries outside Maryland were intended for the lay person rather than for the clergy.

The Philadelphia Library Company, also called the Library Company of Pennsylvania, was an outgrowth of Franklin's philosophical discussion group and debating society, the Junto Literary Club, founded in 1731. (The Junto also generated the America Philosophical Society in 1743.) The Library Company has been called the first circulating library in America. When the Junto decided to start a library, the original plan was for each member to donate books, but this proved unsatisfactory so a subscription library was begun on July 1, 1731. Each member contributed money to purchase books, which were originally kept in the home of one of the members. A librarian,

Louis Timothee, was hired, soon to be replaced by Franklin, who gave each member a catalogue which had been printed at his own expense.[28] The library itself was open to the public to use on the premises, but books circulated only to members,[29] with special borrowing privileges extended to members of Congress, which was then meeting in Independence Hall. Interestingly, when the British occupied Philadelphia, they were accorded borrowing privileges on payment of a deposit.[30] The Library Company soon spawned others, perhaps as many as sixty or more before the Revolution. These were sometimes called proprietary or social libraries. It was also the ever-resourceful Franklin who invented a means of reaching high shelves consisting of a stick with a wire grasping device on the end.

The artisans and tradespeople could sometimes use proprietary libraries in various towns by paying a fee or could use the bookseller's circulating libraries like John Mein's in Boston, which was in existence for several decades before the Revolution and cost £1,8 shillings. (The Library Company's yearly fee was thirty shillings in 1787.) This was too expensive for many so they started their own proprietary libraries, based on Franklin's idea. (These were sometimes called mechanic's libraries.) Soon almost all the larger towns had such libraries, most of which were supposed to be open to the public, but were in reality used primarily by the people who started and supported them—artisans, tradespeople, or professionals.[31]

There was a definite influence of private libraries on the development of public libraries. Some of the wealthy colonial merchants who collected their own libraries, such as Abraham Redwood at Newport, Rhode Island, who specialized in the classics, theology, philosophy, and science, also established public libraries. Redwood's original home library was somewhat open to the public, but in 1747 he gave £500 to establish another library, which was open to the public, although privately owned and maintained. The latter continues in this fashion to the present. The Charleston Library Society was begun in 1748 and the New York Society Library in 1754.

James Logan, secretary and chief justice of Pennsylvania, built Stenton in 1728 in Germantown near Philadelphia, which had a library across the entire front of the house. This library of over 3,000 volumes was the third largest in the colonies at that time. In 1751 Logan left in his will to the city of Philadelphia a building and 3,000 books, plus an endowment for maintenance, to establish a library for public use. Logan's collection itself went to the Library Company in Philadelphia; Benjamin Franklin was to have inventoried the collection, but the inventory has never been found.[32]

College libraries too were important in the general availability of books. By 1700 college library collections generally exceeded those of any private library[33] and were open to "cultivated gentlemen."[34] John Harvard had come to America from England in the late 1630's; he died very soon after arriving in this country and left his library of about 400 books and his estate of nearly £800 to the college later named in his honor. (He did not, of course, found the school, as is sometimes erroneously assumed; he may never even have visited the then unnamed school.) In 1764 the five-thousand-volume library was completely destroyed by fire, but the alumni response was so great in the giving of their own books or money to buy books that the library was soon replaced.[35] Yale received a library from Jeremy Dummer around 1714 which he sent over from England.[36] College students' private libraries often showed that they had (and presumably read) the classic Greek writers.[37]

None of these had any great impact in Virginia. Pre-Revolutionary Virginia relied on England for almost all its goods, including books. There were private collections sometimes that were thrown open to the public through the benevolence of the owners, such as Edward Moseley at Edenton.[38] Similar quasi-public libraries were often found in the South, but the brisk book trade, the library companies, the philanthropy that started public or semi-public libraries, and a college library as prestigious as Harvard or Yale, were lacking.

Thomas Jefferson, of course, had a very fine library at Monticello. Jefferson came from a family of book-owners, his parents having had a library at Shadwell in western Virginia. Jefferson probably had the best private library on architecture in the colonies;[39] when he later sold his books to the Library of

Congress in 1815, he had what was probably the foremost private library in the United States,[40] numbering over 6,000 volumes. Large libraries like the Byrds' and Jefferson's were unusual, but virtually all plantations had a small assortments of books or pamphlets on farming, religion, law, medicine, and politics. Washington's 800 to 1,000 volumes on practical as well as more esoteric subjects was not, as some biographers have insisted, particularly rare, at least among the wealthy classes.

George Washington was born into this milieu in 1732. The upper classes of the time consisted of the gentry, scholars, people of means, the clergy, and government officials, as well as anyone with a university degree. The middle class was made up of merchants, shopkeepers, and freeholders, while the lower classes were servants, slaves, and unskilled laborers,[41] many of whom could not read.[42] The Washington family was upper class but not the very highest. They owned land and slaves from both sides of the family, Augustine Washington's and Mary Ball Washington's; and George's two half brothers from his father's first marriage were sent to England to school.

Cunliffe has noted, perhaps a little cynically, that George and his half brothers needed luck, good investments, and a good marriage to have the wealth to move into the very highest class.[43] Before the Revolution there was still a vague feeling on most people's part that they were English; the upper levels especially still had a strong sense of identity with England, and to this class belonged most of the readers of books.[44] George Washington belonged in or near this group by birth, and he later moved even closer to it after he became the owner of Mount Vernon, where he ordered extensively from his factor in London after selling his crops there.

George, who was the fourth generation of Washingtons in this country, probably expected to go to England to be educated, most likely to Appleby, a preparatory school his half brothers had attended. However, the death of his father when George was eleven seems to have prevented this. The family had land but little ready cash, and the older half brothers received the choicest inheritances. George inherited Ferry Farm on the Rappahannock River, where the family had lived since he was seven, but this was under his mother's control until he came of age. There were four brothers and sisters still at home, and his mother did not send him to Appleby.

Virginia in colonial days was very like England in more than a sense of identification. The largely rural society mirrored in many ways that of rural England. A good many of the people, at least among the wealthy landowners, either had come from England themselves or had ancestors who had, as Washington did. Some still thought of London as their intellectual home. There were still few American books to which George could have been exposed.[45] Fox-hunting was popular, and with huge tracts of land owned by relatively few people, it could be indulged in without obstacle. There was no large leading city—the entire society was essentially rural and lacked the unity and the amenities of a major city.

The various versions of Washington's educational career are not only unsubstantiated but also contradictory. He probably went to school from about age seven until about twelve or fourteen. This may have taken the form of tutoring at home or of attending small local schools run by a clergyman or other educated man, or both.

When the Lees and the Washingtons lived near each other, Richard Henry Lee and George Washington, both age nine, exchanged the following letters:

Richard Henry Lee to George Washington — Pa brought me two pretty books full of pictures he got them in Alexandria they have pictures of dogs and cats and tigers and elefants and ever so many pretty things cousin bids me send you one of them it has a picture of an elefant and a little indian boy on his back like uncle jo's sam pa says if I learn my tasks good he will let uncle jo bring me to see you will you ask your ma to let you come to see me. Richard Henry Lee

George Washington's reply—*Dear Dickey I thank you very much for the pretty picture book you gave me. Sam asked me to show him the pictures and I showed him all the pictures in it; and I read to him*

how the tame Elephant took care of the master's little
boy, and put him on his back and would not let any
touch his master's son. I can read three or four pages
sometimes without missing a word. Ma says I may go
to see you and stay all day with you next week if it be
not rainy. She says I may ride my pony Hero if Uncle
Ben will go with me and lead Hero. I have a little piece
of poetry about the picture book you gave me, but I
mustnt tell you who wrote the poetry.

G.W.'s complements to R.H.L.
And likes his book full well
Henceforth will count him his friend,
And hopes many days he may spend.
      Your good friend, George Washington

The poetry, it is believed, was written by a visitor to the
Washington house, a Mr. Howard.[46]

We can assume that Washington, as well as knowing how
to read and write English (as many did not), knew elementary
Latin, mathematics, the basics of good conduct, a little English
literature, and geography. Later, he learned surveying. This
was not much education by either European or American
standards of the time for the upper class of society. Not only
did he not go to preparatory school in England, but he also did
not attend William and Mary College or some other college, as
might have been expected.

> In short, George Washington was not highly
> educated, and never became what might be called an
> intellectual. Here he is in sharp contrast with
> Americans like John Adams who was later to
> maintain, sourly, "That Washington was not a scholar
> is certain. That he was too illiterate, unlearned,
> unread for his station is equally past dispute."[47]

This view was borne out by Morison who calls Washington's
formal education "scanty" and his schoolmasters "haphazardly
chosen"; "Washington gained little discipline from book-
learning. . . ." Morison points out that a colonial college had a
more demanding curriculum; at least in a classical education,
than is now the case. Washington was a gentleman by birth but

not by education, and this became even more apparent to himself and to others when he went at the age of fourteen or fifteen to live with his half brother, Lawrence, at Mount Vernon.[48] (There is an unsubstantiated story that George lived with his other half brother Augustine for a time. Augustine had a library, so George *might* have been exposed to books while in his early to mid-teens if he really did stay there.) Lawrence had a better education and had traveled enough to enjoy a polish George did not have, and moreover had married a Fairfax of nearby Belvoir, which gave him an entreé into the very best society.

There is strong evidence that George Washington felt a lack of education both in an intellectual and a social sense, was even embarrassed by it, all his life. "He suffered all his life from feeling that he had received an inferior education."[49] Probably he set out to educate himself about this time; this seems to have continued all his life. "We may attribute a little of the constraint of the mature Washington to his awareness of his own intellectual limitations."[50]

In a letter to David Humphreys in 1785 when Washington was fifty-three, he says:

> In a former letter I informed you, my dear Humphreys, that if I had talents for it, I have not leisure to turn my thoughts to commentaries. A consciousness of a defective education, and a certainty of the want of time, unfit me for such a undertaking.

If he still felt his lack of education this much, at fifty-three, after successfully commanding the army during the Revolution, we may assume that the somewhat unsophisticated boy suddenly moving into polished society felt it even more. He was self-conscious about his inability to speak French and later refused to visit France, which his friend the Marquis de LaFayette had been imploring him to do, because he would need an interpreter.[51] He had some facility, however, in Latin, as evidenced by this inscription probably written about 1745 when he would have been thirteen:

*INSCRIPTION ON A FLY LEAF OF A LATIN
TRANSLATION OF HOMER:* "Hunc mihi quaeso
[bone Vir] Libellum Redde, si forsan tenues repertum
Ut Scias qui sum sine fraude Scriptum.
                    Est mihi nomen,
              Georgio Washington
              George Washington
                    Fredericksburg,
                        Virginia."

In approximately this same period we find him writing an
acrostic, which he seems to have had difficulty in finishing:

*ACROSTIC TO "FRANCES ALEXA —"
From your bright sparkling Eyes, I was undone;
Rays, you have more transparent than the sun,
A midst its glory in the rising Day,
None can you equal in your bright array;
Constant in your calm and unspotted Mind;
Equal to all, but will to none Prove kind,
So knowing, seldom one so Young, you'l Find*

*Ah! woe's me, that I should Love and conceal,
Long have I wish'd, but never dare reveal,
Even though severly Loves Pains I feel;
Xerxes that great, was't free from Cupids Dart
And all the greatest Heroes, felt the smart.*

In other matters, however, Washington was not as adept.
His spelling has been the subject of much controversy, with
some insisting that irregular spelling was the rule among even
the well-educated, and others contending that by comparison
with Hamilton, Jefferson, or Franklin, Washington's spelling
was inferior.[52] Woodward insists that it is erroneous to assume
no one could spell properly until well into the 1800's. Well-
educated people, he says, did spell well and use good grammar.[53] There is some evidence that Washington's spelling
improved with age, but as he later employed letter-writers (to
write from his dictation), this is hard to assess. Spelling is not
an absolute test of mental ability, however, and in the matter of
his actual intellectual attainment, there is again considerable

disagreement. He is so closely associated with "the father of our country" image that it is hard to determine just what his effect on the intellectual and patriotic thought of the time actually was. His letters indicate a considerable ability, but it must be remembered that his achievements were more in "doing," such as commanding the Revolutionary Army, farming his beloved Mount Vernon, or holding the office of first president, in which undertaking his talent may have been for appointing well-qualified people to the various high offices. The actual written documents of the Revolutionary period were not the work of Washington. He was never the brilliant writer that Jefferson and Madison were. His diaries, rather than recording his feelings, expectations, or ideas, tell where he went, what he did, and whom he met.[54] His handwriting has been much praised for its neatness and uniformity[55] but is difficult for the modern reader to decipher.

While the young Washington was living with Lawrence at Mount Vernon, there was a steady round of visiting with nearby Belvoir, home of Colonel William Fairfax and of his son, George William Fairfax, whose sister, Anne Fairfax, married Lawrence Washington, and at Greenway Court, home of Thomas, Lord Fairfax. It is not well substantiated that Lord Fairfax at Greenway Court directed George's choice of books from his library. Almost certainly George William Fairfax of Belvoir and Fairfax's wife, Sally Cary, formed a strong bond of friendship; Sally Cary Fairfax may have encouraged George Washington to read in the library at Belvoir.[56] Washington read Addison's *Cato* with Sally Fairfax, possibly acted it out in private theatricals, and years later at Valley Forge arranged a performance of *Cato* to help boost the morale of the men. He fairly frequently quoted from *Cato* in his letters to Sally Fairfax and to others from then on. When Washington was about seventeen, he owned an English language outline of Seneca's *Dialogues*. The chapter headings alone may have influenced him in later life,[57] but it is rarely possible to determine just what effect a book has actually had on a person who reads it. The chapter headings will, at any rate, show the sort of thing Washington was apparently reading and studying:

An Honest Man can never be outdone in Courtesy
A Good man can never be Miserable, nor a Wicked
   man Happy
A Sensual Life is a Miserable Life
Hope and Fear are the Bane of Human Life
The Contempt of Death makes all the Miseries of Life
   Easy to us

Once when Washington was despondent, Colonel Fairfax consoled him with references to *Caesar's Commentaries*, which Washington apparently had, and to Quintus Curtius, the author of a life of Alexander the Great which Washington may have had.[58]

One very interesting book that Washington was fond of as a boy was a popular English title by W. Mather called *The Young Man's Companion.* This extremely helpful little book told one how to read; write; figure; measure land and lumber; survey; navigate; build houses; plant; treat illness; write wills, deeds, and legal forms; act in society; and make ink. Washington seems to have used this book a great deal, for the pages show much use and some parts have been copied out.[59] In it we may see reflected what much of Washington's library was later like, as well as the kinds of things he was interested in all his life, characterized by the words "eminently practical" (see Illustration 1).

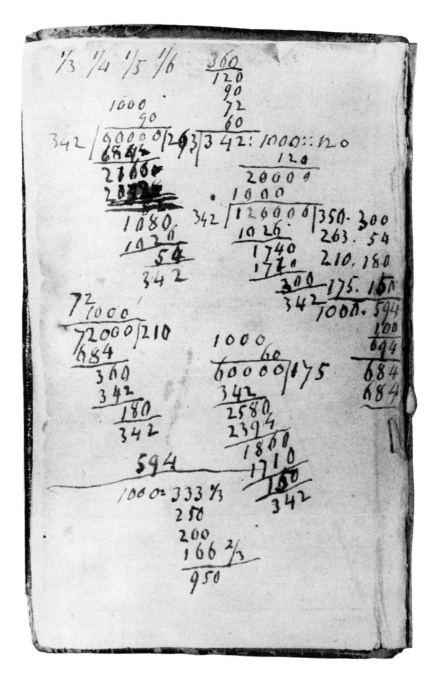

I. Washington's figuring on his copy of **The Young Man's Companion.**

CHAPTER II

The Architecture and Interior Decoration of the Library

George Washington lived in the structure which was to become known as Mount Vernon for four years as a child. His father, Augustine, probably built the one-and-a-half story house about 1735,[1] when the family moved there from Bridge Creek (or Pope's Creek), now known as Wakefield, where George was born (see Illustration 1). The land surrounding Mount Vernon had been owned by three generations of the Washington family before Lawrence, half brother of George Washington, inherited and occupied the house, then known as Little Hunting Creek, in 1743. The land grant to the Washingtons was direct from the grantee of the Crown, Lord Culpepper. The initials, LW, on a cornerstone found on the site are those of George Washington's grandfather. It is known that some form of dwelling was needed on the land to keep the grant. It is believed that Augustine built the central portion of the present house on the site and over the foundation of the "quarter" built by his father in the period 1690-1698.[2] When George was seven, the family moved to Ferry Farm on the Rappahannock River; but after the death of his father, when George was eleven, George was a frequent visitor in Lawrence's home and took up residence there.

Lawrence renamed Little Hunting Creek Plantation after the famous Admiral Vernon with whom he had served in the Royal Navy in the West Indies. The "Mount" came from the land's eminence above the Potomac, named River of Swans by the Indians. It was on this site the house was placed. Lawrence died of tuberculosis in 1752 after a trip to Barbados where he attempted to regain his health. George had accompanied him.

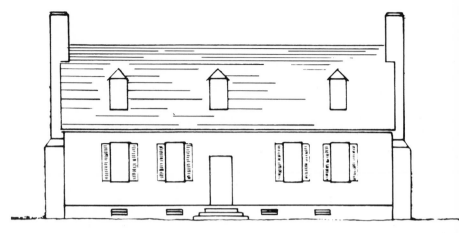

1. Sketch of story-and-a-half cottage, Mount Vernon. An artist's view of original house, reconstructed from data found in Washington's writings and from evidence derived from architectural studies of Mount Vernon today.

Augustine Washington had indicated in his will that George should be the next heir of Mount Vernon if Lawrence died without issue. Lawrence, however, had an infant daughter, Sarah, to whom he left the estate, with a life interest to his wife, Ann Fairfax Washington. Sarah died shortly thereafter. Ann Fairfax remarried and leased Mount Vernon to George permanently. The estate became his in 1761 upon his sister-in-law's death.

George Washington said, *"No estate is more pleasantly situated."* Mount Vernon is located between the Potomac and Rappahannock Rivers, part of an area known as Northern Neck. When Lawrence in 1752 willed Mount Vernon, the area was 2,500 acres. Mansion House Farm accounted for 500 acres. Mount Vernon now covers an area that approximates the boundaries of the Mansion House Farm of Washington's lifetime. The first purchase to restore the estate by the Mount Vernon Ladies' Association of the Union was for 202 acres. The wide sweep of the river of Washington's time has only recently been secured against apartment buildings. The legislation for completion of Piscataway Park on the Potomac River opposite Mount Vernon was passed in 1974 after fifteen years of support from the Association (see Illustration 2).

The style of Mount Vernon spans three American architectural periods: Colonial, ending in 1720; Georgian, ending in 1780; and Federal, ending in 1820. The numerous remodelings initiated by George Washington contributed the features that brought recognition to Mount Vernon as being architecturally significant. He was the sole proprietor for nearly half a century, 1754-1799. He was responsible for the Mansion House Farm's becoming a gentleman's country seat in the English manner with gardens, lawns, groves, meadows, woods, and experimental plots.

The mansion has eighteen or nineteen rooms, depending on whether the central hall, for example, and the pantry are counted, and four or five closets or small rooms. At Mount Vernon there were thirty buildings besides the mansion: an office, kitchen, butler's house, gardener's house, smoke house, wagon shed, milk house, shelter house in the deer park, wharf pavilion, lodge houses at the gates, coach house, barn, summer house, corn house, spring house, wash house, and seven cabins for employees (see Illustration 2).

2. Panoramic View of the Potomac River and Mount Vernon.

The exact date when Washington first occupied Mount Vernon is not known, but a letter dated March 15, 1755, is headed Mount Vernon. When George Washington assumed the responsibility for Mount Vernon in 1754, the new master was a bachelor of twenty-two, engaged in the French and Indian Wars for five years; and Mount Vernon was a typical Southern Colonial house, thirty-two feet deep and forty-eight feet long, with a four-square floor plan and a central hall. There were probably a few outbuildings on the grounds. In the spring of 1754, Mount Vernon appeared like a recruiting station.[3] While George was on the Western Frontier, his younger brother, John, managed the property. Mount Vernon was occasionally occupied, but George Washington led no ordered life and there was none of the development of Mount Vernon that was to come.

He started the remodeling work on Mount Vernon in 1757 before his marriage to Martha Dandridge Custis, a wealthy widow, in 1759. His marriage began his longest, uninterrupted residence, 1759-1775, at Mount Vernon. He devoted his time closely to Mount Vernon and the four working farms: River Farm, Muddy Hole Farm, Union Farm, and Dogue Run Farm, acting as his own general overseer until 1764 when Lund Washington, his second cousin, became his assistant. Except for summers when the farm work was heavy, Washington spent time fox-hunting, fishing, and visiting. Tobacco and wheat were the major crops. Besides producing for home consumption, a fishery and flour mill produced commercially. The intention of Washington to experiment with seeds and fertilizers was always evident. By 1790 he had reached his objective in land ownership, partially from the wills of his father and Lawrence: 5,000 acres of the original grant and another 3,000 adjoining it. Over 3,000 acres were cultivated. Mansion House Farm was not intensely tilled (see Illustration 3).

In the first years of colonial living the poorest kind of provision for shelter was satisfactory, but the desire for the ornamental styles of Europe to which the colonists were accustomed determined housing designs as soon as they prospered

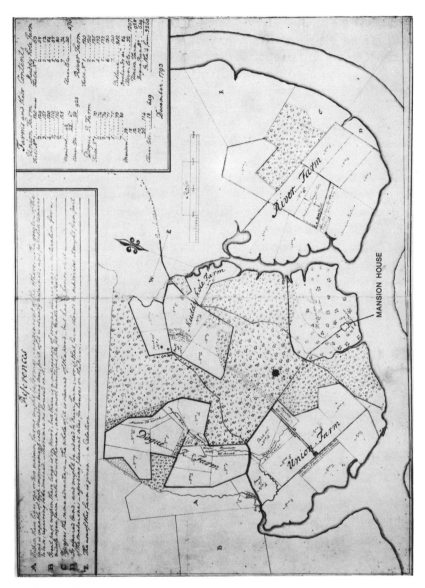

3. George Washington called his map a "rude sketch." It was drawn to assist his effort to rent the farms in 1793. The mansion is the fiddle-shaped mark.

in the new land. The extremes of the weather in the New World necessitated more attention to heating and cooling than had been necessary in Europe. The mornings in Virginia were close and foggy, the evenings cloudy and sometimes rainy; and at nights there were heavy dews. Days were warm and sultry in summer and extremely cold for a part of the winter. Wood instead of stone was the most plentiful building material in America. Early building was circumscribed by these factors, and Mount Vernon was not an exception. The framing of the house was rough-hewn oak; the sheathing, pine, one and one-eighth inches thick, cut from trees grown on the plantation. The roof shingles were cypress, hand-shaped.[4] The asymmetrical position of the windows to the right and left of the west entry door in the first structure was typical of early casual building or haphazard additions to buildings (see Illustration 1). The number of freedoms given a builder lessened after 1700 as the unmistakably more formal styles became popular. Washington made a major decision in deciding to remodel rather than build anew.

One of the characteristics of Southern Colonial architecture was the positioning of chimneys in the ends of the house, which was unlike the popular styles of the North, the saltbox and the Cape Cod, which utilized a central chimney near the center of the house. The fireplace became a symbol of wealth as brick replaced a mixture of clay and twigs. Some home owners had a fireplace in each room and used one chimney for two or more fireplaces in adjoining rooms (see Illustration 4). George Washington estimated the number of bricks, planks, shingles, etc., that would be needed for the remodeling himself and some of the bricks were made in his kilns. In addition to rebuilding the fireplaces and putting the structure on a brick foundation in 1758-1759, he had the roof raised, increasing the number of rooms to twelve. Many Virginia houses follow the full eight-room-and-attic plan, lifting the structure to the plan if not the proportions of the central "great" house.[5]

When the second full floor was added, the outside of Mount Vernon was covered with new boards, beveled to ap-

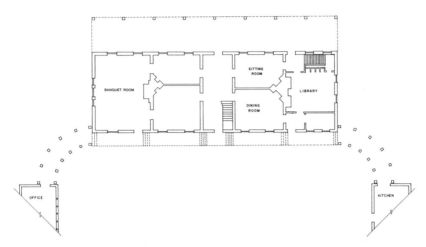

4. The plan for unity of buildings through the use of colonnades is quite clear. There are inaccuracies in an early drawing done by George Washington such as nine pillars on the piazza instead of eight. The artist retained the nine pillars but corrected the colonnades' position, which Washington had shown joining the house at exact right angles, and added the position of the book press and fireplace but not the inner wall of the pantry or the restored closet.

pear rusticated, a popular treatment in imitation of stone (see Color Plate I). George Washington wrote to William Thornton, gentleman architect, in 1799:

> Sanding is designed to answer two purposes, durability, and presentation of Stone; for the latter purpose, and in my opinion a desirable one; it is the last operation, by dashing, as long as any will stick, the Sand upon a coat of thick paint.

Washington acted as contractor for all his buildings for labor and supplies. He paid Ł328 (equal to $1500) September 15, 1759, for "Patterson's work on house including all charges against me to this day" which was for about two years work. Patterson was "undertaker" or the builder. The following order was to Robert Cary and Company to secure materials from England:

Mount Vernon, October 6, 1773
Gentn: I am almost ashamed to trouble you, in the
same year, with such frequent Orders for Goods; but
as I am under a necessity of making some repairs to,
and alterations in my House, and did not get an Acct.
before from the Undertaker of all the Materials
wanting it must plead my Excuse for requesting you to
send me the undermentioned Articles. . . .

For Geo: Washington
100 Sqrs. of best Crown Glass 9 by 11
A Cask of Whiting
400 Wt. of White Lead ground in Oyl
over and above the last Order.
30 lb red Lead. 2 lb Lampblack
100 lb yellow Oaker. 10 lb Umber
20 Gallns. best Brittish Lintseed Oyl
for Inside painting
9 pr. dovetail Mortice Hinges mid: size
3 pr. Ditto larger
9 Comm. brass cased Locks 3 Do dble. Spd. best Do
3 M 2d.   Brads 3 M 3d.   Do 6 M 4d.   Do
6 M 6d. Do 8 M Clasp Nails instead of Brads for
Flooring
40 M 4d. Nails 100 lbs of Lead for Windows
and 50 fathom Sash Line.
25 Lbs. best Glew ½ a Ton of unprepd. Plaist'r of
Paris

The early Americans lavished money on their homes, attempting to enlarge them to make them monumental. Colonial architecture was usually a generation behind the mother country; however, the decorative, bold massing of the new Georgian style when it reached the colonies suited the robust, confident culture of the day.[6] The Georgian house had a balanced facade, usually four windows down and five up. After 1750 when the central hall became a feature of houses in the North as well as the South, the most common floor plan associated with the Georgian style was the four square, central hall. The central hall at Mount Vernon originally had a partition which divided it into a front and rear hall.[7] In the early improvements the hall was extended front to back to form the typical Southern floor plan of which it was said no house was too small for the formality of the central hall. Part of the appeal of the Georgian style was the satisfying proportions. Embellishments similar to that on the outside doors and windows were placed on interior doors and windows (see Color Plate II).

The Georgian houses were situated parallel to the road. Mount Vernon utilized both the drive *and* the dock to receive people.

> When there were guests to be put over the river . . .
> between Mount Vernon and Warburton Manor . . .
> long boats, manned by liveried slaves in checkered
> shirts and black velvet caps, would set out from each
> side for the middle of the river where they met and the
> passengers changed boats.[9]

Some aspects of the Georgian style came from Renaissance Italy. Andrea Palladio, 1508-1580, had used colonnades to unite landscape and house, and the idea to connect outbuildings with the main mass at right angles by colonnades was carried out at Mount Vernon (see Illustration 4). The colonnades have become one of the best known architectural features of Mount Vernon (see Color Plate III). *"I am not skilled in architecture . . ."* George Washington wrote in 1798, but Palladio's publication in translation as well as other books of architecture and manuals of carpentry were available to him. The books of architecture created an extremely high standard of knowledge among all builders, one of the great artistic accomplishments of the eighteenth century.[10] Architecture was part of the education and interest of a gentleman; but, in addition, Washington was trained as a surveyor and was familiar with drawing tools. In the early years, however, he never drew to scale.

It is speculated that Washington may have gotten the idea for the piazza from the early trip to the West Indies. Nothing like it was known to have been used on contemporary or earlier buildings in that part of the country and is thought to be original with Washington. The piazza employed eight square columns instead of the Greek columns that began to be extremely popular as Georgian architecture waned. The pediment that was customarily attached to the Greek columns was placed on the west front of Mount Vernon. Washington split the two prominent and popular features of the newest architectural style (compare Color Plates I and III). Benjamin Henry Latrobe, an eminent architect of the time, said of Mount Vernon in 1796 after visiting there, "It has no very striking appearance, though superior to every other house I have seen here."[12]

After the Peace of Utrecht threw open the seas, more workmen were available. Going Lanphire or Gawen Lamphier, at Mount Vernon, was a competent workman in some respects; but Washington wrote July, 1774, the work ". . . *goes on better whilst I am present, than in my absence from the workmen . . .*" and August 20, 1775, "*I wish you would quicken Lanphier and Sears . . .*" He would have been more discouraged if he had known then how much time he would be required to be away from Mount Vernon in the next ten years.

The work on the second major enlargement of Mount Vernon went slowly. Washington drew his plans in 1773 for the library, one of the two additions to the main mass, the library to be on the south end and a banquet hall on the north end, the latter to increase the number of public rooms. In the Georgian period the library seems to have achieved the best physical representation and the truest emphasis on its primary purpose. The library was positioned for immediate access, yet was quiet, providing the atmosphere associated with cultural pursuits and extending hospitality. The library had a prestigious location, usually at the left or right of the main entrance on the first floor. In the South placing the kitchen outside the main block was quite likely since that reduced the risk of fire and the annoyance of flies or odors. This increased the chances that one of the two rooms not used for a dining room or living room would be devoted to a library. If Washington had followed the usual plan, he would have placed the library on the first floor either in the area designated the music room or the downstairs bedroom. Washington made the decision in 1759 to place a bed in one of the downstairs rooms. The family consisted always of George and Martha and her two children as a minimum number, and the house never seemed to offer sufficient room for the family. In planning the enlargement he did not know his needs for his later years, but he had lived at Mount Vernon for a sufficient time to have thought about the need for space to meet his present needs. Later, the guests were so numerous that Washington once laughingly referred to his house as ". . . *a well-resorted tavern . . .*" Uninvited guests were not refused hospitality in Virginia by gentlemen. The amount of space devoted to bedrooms at Mount Vernon seems to respect this courtesy. George Washington once wrote that he and Martha had not sat down alone to a dinner for twenty years. At one time when Washington was in residence, as many as ninety people were regular occupants of the mansion, in its wing buildings, and in the buildings in the service lanes. Overseers, secretaries, maids, stablemen, waiters, cooks, drivers, semptresses, spinners, washers, gardeners, carpenters, knitters, carters, smiths, and their families accounted for the large number.

The decision that a room be used as a library in a private home is determined by need, by wealth, or by whim of the owner. The country gentlemen of America tried to live like the cultured gentlemen of England. An English country house would probably have had a library. For example, in June, 1753, Walpole wrote to a friend that he was planning to build at Strawberry Hill, a library, 20x30x15; he refers to it as one of only two good chambers he shall have in the house in Twickenham, England.[13] The library wing at Mount Vernon is 22x33x11 and the library is 19.2x16.8x10.9. Also included in the second expansion was the outside kitchen on the south. In addition to the usual slowness of building, this period of time was extremely busy for Washington—sitting for a portrait by Peale, the making of a bust by Houdon, the death of a stepchild, his attendance at the House of Burgesses in Williamsburg, and the visit of two former British army men who were rivals of his for military authority.[14] Usually the house plans would have been neater and more detailed. The plans for the separate kitchen were not drawn because he had expected to be there. Lund Washington was the overseer for the work while Washington was away. Sometimes a decision beyond the workmen or needed materials would be supplied by a neighbor.

The exterior of the library was framed before he left in May, 1775, for Philadelphia and the Second Continental Congress. The lumber for the new north wing of the house was stacked.

> . . . if I could be furnished with one thousand feet of the best pine plank, precisely 24 feet long when dressed, to be without knots or sap. It is for the floor of my new room. Many years ago I provided for this, and thought myself secure of that which was perfectly seasoned. It had been dressed and laid by; but when I was about to make use of it, behold! two thirds of it was stolen, and the other ⅓ will match no plank I can now get.

Washington saw the work only once during the time of his war service, 1775-1781; this was during his march to Yorktown, as Commander-in-Chief of the Army.

The completion of the interior of the library, with the exception of the built-in bookshelves, before the end of 1775, was probably due to the lesser amount of decoration rather than to any urgency of need. However, the legacy of English home living was supported in the South by the plantation home being the center of business as well. Rather than a shop or office in the town, the library room provided the needed office space.

No room in the mansion is more intimately associated with Washington's life at Mount Vernon than the library.[15] In his library he tallied his accounts, looked at crop reports, and wrote the letters that shaped history. Comments from his diary indicate his need, perhaps desire, for a library in which to work:

June 24, 1771	*At home all day writing.*
June 26, 1771	*At home all day writing.*
December 23, 1771	*At home all day writing and alone.*
December 24, 1771	*At home all day and writing as yesterday—alone.*
December 1, 1772	*At home all day a Writing to Williamsburg.*
February 16, 1774	*At home all day alone—being engaged in writing.*

He carried a small pocket-book in which he kept figures. He ordered in 1760 one which cost £1 and was delivered on the *Sarah Rush* out of London:

> . . . *very neat Pocket Book-7 inches long and 4½ wide with several Vellom or other Leaves that will bear writing Thereon with a Pencil & rubbing out again-so have a Pencil therein, & a Pocket or two for Paper-to be inclosed & fastened by a Silver Catch.*

The managers of his farms reported to Washington's manager on Saturdays. These reports were set in order and passed on to Washington who transcribed them into his notebooks, diaries, and accounts.[16] When he was away, he required a report from his manager by post leaving Alexandria each Thursday. He usually devoted Sunday afternoon to long letters back, first in rough draft, then copied in his own writing and then preserved with a letter-press copy. These letters had a certain intimacy as though he were in his library in a talk with his manager after a morning ride of inspection.[17] Usage of the library was continuous, routine. In the library the letters were received that daily came for him from all over the world and here also the letters were written that carried the political views to every other state. After dinner he withdrew with guests to the library occasionally, and in the library he made a hasty survey of the newspapers of which he received a great many.

> *To Clement Biddle, Philadelphia*
> *February 1, 1785*
> *I do not know how to account for it, but so the fact is, that altho I am a Subscriber to Messrs. Dunlap and Claypoole's Packet and Daily Advertiser, I do not get one paper in five of them . . . let me know the cause of my disappointments . . .*

Mount Vernon is restful, dignified, and well-built. Washington said, *"Nothing but durable materials shall be used in this house."* In addition, the house was designed with taste and restraint. He had little time, money, or information with which to work. Although his ownership of Mount Vernon covered forty-five years, the periods of time in residence, in which he could become actively involved in the estate, were few. During the time he was president he spent fifteen months of the eight years at home. After the presidency he spent his last two years, 1797-1799, in retirement at Mount Vernon, where he died. He was not wealthy and money was often invested rather than free for his plans or projects.

> *To Lund Washington, Newburgh [New York]*
> *February 12, 1783*
> *I want to know before I come home [as I shall come home with empty pockets whenever Peace shall take place] how Affairs stand with me, and what my dependence is.*

In a letter to his sister-in-law in 1798 he wrote,

> *I will answer for purchases made in this manner, to the amount of a thousand dollars, but am unable to advance more, and this indeed will be drawn from a use to which it was actually appropriated.*

He did have access to the known information but the slowness of communication in the colonies did not bring new styles to rural areas quickly. Mount Vernon seems to have been a result of George Washington's practical adaptation of the current modes to his individual problem. His taste was sound enough to prevent his acceptance of anything extreme.[18]

That he did give serious thought to the placement and design of the library is easily ascertained from his plan to connect the library by a stairway to his bedroom above. The major doors of the library connect the library with two small hallways but not directly with other rooms of the house, all of which gave him a wing that could be relatively private. *"As it is my inclination to retire [and unless prevented by very particular company, I always do retire] either to bed or to my study soon after candlelight . . ."* In the South a meal (referred to as tea or dinner) was served at 3 P.M. and supper was served at nine. George Washington usually returned from his inspection of crops, dressed, and partook of the three o'clock meal, conversing afterwards. He spent perhaps two hours writing in the evening. He often did not eat at the later meal although it was prepared and served for the household. He frequently retired to bed at nine.

An outside entrance was generally used by professional men, such as lawyers, doctors, and clergymen, who kept their offices in their homes. These rooms were often studies or libraries and were in an ell of the house which kept their professional and family life separated. The library at Mount Vernon was accessible from either the southwest or southeast exterior doors. The arrangement of the doors in these small entryways reveals a special problem Washington encountered in the addition of this wing. The door to the library from the east entry hall opens into the library and actually hits the corner of the chair railing on the chimney. Both major doors into the library, when open, obscure the cupboards on either side of the fireplace. The library doors have to be closed in order to open the cupboard doors to get at whatever was stored there. The east entry has only three doors and the stairwell, since the small storage area on the north wall of that entry faces into the downstairs bedroom, providing a two-doored cupboard for the bedroom. There are six doors in the west entry at the present time, including one to a small cupboard. The restored closet added one more. Physical evidence clearly reveals that Washington had framed two door openings in the south wall of the west entry. One was closed and completely plastered over at some later period. The door, as Washington planned it, entered a small closet which provided space for his out-of-door clothing and accessories. The door opening and closet were restored in 1962 (see Illustrations 4 and 5).

Ordinarily the architectural style chosen for the exterior of a house will dictate such interior features as the type of window, ceiling, or doorway. Several of the rooms of Mount Vernon, the banquet room and the west parlor especially, do follow this assumption. The library at Mount Vernon seems to have less evidence of the ornate style that appears in the other rooms. Certainly the library appears very plain when compared with the banquet room which was planned at the same time as the library. The ceiling of the library is lower, measuring only 10.9 feet. The increase in the heights of ceilings was a principal

5. The two doors of the pantry and the reconstructed closet. A platter can be seen through the window placed on the interior wall, upper left center of the photograph.

feature of Georgian architecture. The ceiling height went from six feet in colonial times to eighteen in the Federal Period. Early colonial ceilings were often beamed and whitewashed. Plaster ceilings were more often plain than decorated, but some of the fine homes decorated the ceilings with figures in relief. The ceiling of the banquet room has a geometric design of agricultural symbols and Adam sunbursts; and the ceilings of the west parlor and the dining room are decorated so beautifully as to rival any in the area.[19] The plaster at Mount Vernon was made from oyster shells from the bed of the river which is said to have given it a chalky appearance.[20] The library has a plain, plastered ceiling and a cornice for decoration. The ceiling cornice design has a relatively simple Greek motif, not repeated in other rooms at Mount Vernon but used again on the fireplace in the library, appearing one and one-eighth inch in size there. Since the ceiling is lower in this room, the panel molding is touching the cornice on the north wall (see Color Plate IV).

The library at Mount Vernon loses much drama from the poor locations of the entries into it, a circumstance directly related to its being an addition to an existing structure. An entrance is best from a main hall, possibly through double doors, each slightly narrower than a regular door, or a single door of generous proportions. A door should open on the most magnificent and extensive prospect of a room. At Mount Vernon the person entering the library from either entrance sees a room without balance, partially due to the person being parallel with the fireplace as he enters, and partially due to the bookshelves, the only other heavy, built-in feature in the room besides the fireplace, being at a right angle to the fireplace, rather than opposite the fireplace.

The placement of the fireplace, since it is both an attraction and a service, should be opposite the entry or in the line of vision as the door of the library opens since the fireplace is a focal point for the gathering of people. The very sight of fire adds to a room a kind of reputation.[21] At his receptions in Philadelphia an eyewitness says President Washington always stood in front of the fireplace, with his face toward the door of entrance.[22] However, Washington had no other way to arrange his library room since the fireplace shared a chimney with two other rooms of the original structure and the windows were fixed on the only outside wall. Washington probably also lost the comfort of a chair by the fire because the area was really a walkway between the two doors in his time as well as at the present time.

That he built shelves for his books on only one wall seems to indicate a preconceived notion of the size of the collection since his house plans in almost every case previously had been characterized by balance, equal size, and formality. For example, George Washington wrote, *"The chimney in the new room should be exactly in the middle of it—the doors and every thing else to be exactly answerable and uniform—. . ."* Many libraries use all of the wall space for shelving, leaving only the doors and windows free. Shelves on the west *and* east walls would have retrieved some of the sense of entering a traditional library room. The plan of Washington for shelves on one wall precludes any thought that the room was too formal or possessed too little of the individuality of the owner. Although used primarily as an office, the atmosphere of the library was not totally "business" as a result of his using wall space to accommodate the desk and choosing a desk which had shelving for books above the writing surface.

All colonists probably felt as Washington did about the possible loss of possessions by fire. *"There is nothing that fills my mind with more apprehension when I am from home than fire,"* he said in 1791. He had six leather fire buckets in the house and buckets of salt in the attic to be poured down a chimney flue if it caught fire.[23] The fire buckets bore the name of George Washington and were made in Philadelphia. Jefferson had used the mantel for shelving his books in his home, a very unwise procedure; but there is no evidence of this at Mount Vernon as an early means of storage before the built-in bookshelves in the library were installed. The mantelpiece was not common in early colonial houses and began to appear after the first quarter of the eighteenth century.[24] The mantelpiece in the library at Mount Vernon is six inches in width and on it are placed two candle holders, which are representative of the colonial period of home decoration but have no provenance, authentic documentation of having ever been pieces used at

Mount Vernon. The andirons, shovel, etc., are period pieces also (see Color Plate IV). The inventory did list tongs, shovel, and fender. A pole or fire screen may have been used, but its placement by the fireplace would have been almost an obstacle in the traffic pattern between the two library doors which exists for tourists today and which is very similar to that of Washington's time.

Wood was most often the material used for mantels, resulting in hand-carved decoration. The design on the mantel in the library at Mount Vernon is not overshadowed by the window or door decoration. A wide piece of black marble was used as facing for the fireplace in the library. This extraordinarily wide facing, measuring thirteen to fourteen inches rather than the normal six to eight inches, was used to cover the second fireplace opening that Lund had made in attempting to correct the vexing smoking condition by reducing the size of the fireplace opening (see Color Plate IV). The library fireplace burned wood, as did most of the twelve in the house, with the exception being the one in the banquet room which burned coal.

The Italian marble and jasper mantel in the banquet room was a gift from Samuel Vaughan, a wealthy London merchant and an ardent supporter of the American cause. The mantel had been used in Vaughan's library in Wanstead, England, but Washington placed it in the banquet room saying, "*I greatly fear it is too elegant and costly for my room, and republican stile of living.*" Marble mantels were imported only after the Revolution. Washington's gift arrived in ten cases in 1785, just as the second frost set in, which delayed delivery by water. Transportation overland nine miles was considered too hazardous (see Color Plate V).

The picture above the library fireplace mantel, entitled *A Hunting Piece,* may be one that was listed on the inventory of personal things that Washington had made when he left Philadelphia upon retirement from the presidency (see Color Plate IV). The title of the picture happens to be too general for the evidence to be conclusive although the name on the Philadelphia list was given as *A Hunting Piece.* In the later inventories of other rooms the names of pictures were often given. In the library, however, only one of the two pictures on the inventory is listed by name, the portrait of Lawrence Washington. The portrait of his half-brother is known to have been at Mount Vernon while George Washington was there. It is not known who the artist is, and the picture is said to lack finesse.[25] The portrait, thirty by twenty-five inches, shows a man from the waist up (see Color Plate IX). Portraits are traditional over the fireplace mantel in a library, but the size of the portrait of Lawrence prevents it being placed there.

Molding designs above and below the mantelpiece of a fireplace were kept similar until 1790. The panel outlined by molding above the mantelpiece in the library at Mount Vernon is the same size, shape, and type as in several other rooms at Mount Vernon. Almost any oddments on the shelf would infringe on the decoration placed within the outlines of the molding above the shelf (see Color Plate IV). The size and color of the picture chosen to hang over the fireplace is well-suited to the area outlined by the molding, and the two candle holders do not impinge on the panel or its decoration.

The English horn for fox-hunting which hangs to the left of the mantel bears an engraving, Piccadilly, London. It is an authentic Mount Vernon piece. Nothing has been placed on the right of the mantel to give balance (see Color Plate IV). Girandole (candle holders) on each side of a fireplace are often used but not at Mount Vernon. Washington referred to *"gerandole"* which consisted of brackets and mirrors, but not with attached candle holders, for the banquet room. There is very little wall space in the library suitable for any wall decoration by present standards, but pictures were hung above doorways then.

There are four doors in the library, each approximately six feet six inches in height, with six panels, the latter a characteristic of Georgian architecture. The simple batten doors of colonial days had become more sophisticated, with two to three panels, later four to six. The doorways in some of the rooms at Mount Vernon have heavy pediments, even more ornate than the central doors on the west and east exteriors. Broken pediments were the most popular at the time and were also used over fireplaces as in the west parlor. The doorways in the library are without any decoration except the simple design created by the grooved surface of the molding of the frames. The molding is six inches wide and mitered, forming a clean right angle at the corners unlike the ears created by the molding around the black marble of the fireplace (compare Color Plates IV and VII). Two of the doors are on the east wall, one either side of the built-in bookshelves, flush with their glass doors. The smaller of the two doors leads to a closet under the stairs that served to give Washington additional storage, possibly for a *"fireskreen,"* one that appears to have been odd, as the others are listed in pairs on the inventory. At the time of Washington's death Mount Vernon had three pairs of fire screens. The pair listed as being in the banquet room was valued at $40. Two pairs were listed in the *"Lumber room"* or storeroom in the garret.

A library in a home is used individually and can be somewhat isolated for that reason; it is one room that must be capable of being shut off as it is a place of contemplation and solitude. George Washington was known during a part of his life to rise at 4:00 A.M. and go the library to work until breakfast at 7:00 A.M. He often made his own fire in the library fireplace in the morning. After a breakfast of Indian cakes, honey, and tea or coffee, he would go to the stables to start the day's inspection trip. The dressing table in the library at Mount Vernon and a copper wash basin listed on the room's inventory seem believable under these circumstances, but the dressing table was restored to the library only as recently as 1975 although available long before that time (see Illustration 6). People until recently were unwilling to accept the untraditional in the library, even though this piece of furniture was known to have been kept in Washington's study during his lifetime. He paid £19 for the *"large shaving & dressing table"* and willed it to his friend Dr. David Stuart, who married the widow of John Parke Custis, Washington's step-son. In 1905 it was purchased from one of Dr. Stuart's descendants and restored to Mount Vernon. It is now displayed closed with china shaving accessories on the top.

A library is, however, also used for the reception of visitors. Its relationship to other rooms which open into it then

6. Dressing Table. Mahogany; marble top,
   mirror inset. France, ca. 1775-85.

becomes a matter of concern. The arrangement of Mount
Vernon provided for George Washington's need to be away
from people but lessened the usefulness of the library for social
purposes. Two doors of the same size (approximately thirty-six
inches in width) lead to small hallways, east and west. The west
area was devoted primarily to food service. The pantry adjoining the library was unusual and perhaps a distracting
element since quietness is as essential as light for reading. A
cellar-kitchen under the library had a layer of lath and plaster
applied directly to the underside of the library floor as well as a

plastered ceiling. The handmade lath nails indicate that this was done during the initial period of the wing's construction possibly to insure protection from the noise of activities, odors, or drafts of the cellar. Washington may have been away from the house when a great deal of the preparation of meals was done, or dressing for dinner or greeting guests before dinner in another room of the house. He enjoyed the *"cheerful converse of the social board,"*[26] and may not have considered the preparations for a meal a disturbance. The pantry also should be viewed as more the serving area than the preparation area.

The pantry is divided into two parts. A small door of the library opens directly into the southern half of the pantry; and the closeness of the pantry for serving a glass of wine in the library could be a convenience, but not one, seemingly, utilized by Washington. Natural light into this part of the pantry is supplied by the interior window placed over the door (see Illustration 5), the light actually coming from a west exterior window in the northern half of the pantry. The kitchen, the pantry, and the family dining room are arranged conveniently for that period of time; but the banquet room was a considerable distance from the source of food and drink. Servants, besides walking the distance from the kitchen to the house, had to step up and down, one step at the kitchen doorway, two at the colonnade, three at the main entrance, etc. (see Illustration 4).

The view from the library windows of the landscaping that Washington had achieved may have given him a great deal of enjoyment. Much of the charm of Mount Vernon lies in its graceful situation in its environment. George Washington had purchased *New Principles of Gardening* by Batty Langley in 1759 which said, "shady walks (should) be planted from the End-views of a House and terminate in . . . Groves."[27] Washington followed this advice (see Color Plate VI). However, the room has never been arranged to show an easy chair near the windows for one to use either to enjoy the view or the light for reading. The roof of the shed that covers the steps to the cellar would intrude on the view toward the Potomac from the southeast window of the library for anyone but a tall person like Washington (see Color Plate III).

Washington enjoyed the library, his favorite room. It was a bright sunny room, somewhat small, and not furnished with many chairs and without a sofa. Mount Vernon was situated so that each side admitted sunlight at some time during the day. The comfort seems minimal while the function of the room as an office appears to be of more importance.

He kept there his personal possessions: a cane, a gun for ducking on the Potomac, an iron chest, a barometer, and a terrestrial globe, all of which are kept in the library today. Washington's diary often noted the weather:

May 2, 1760	*Cold, and strong westerly Winds,*
March 4, 1797	*Much such a day as yesterday in all respects. Mercury at 41.*
September 20, 1772	*At home all day. Weather clear and Warm, with but little Wind.*

The gold head or cap on the tall walking stick is original and has the Washington coat of arms on it. This cane is the one given by the Mount Vernon Ladies' Association to Edward Everett in 1858 and returned by his granddaughter in 1911. (Everett gave a series of lectures on Washington to raise money for the original purchase of Mount Vernon by the Association.) The ducking gun is the longer one in the corner (see Color Plate VII). A number of surveying compasses have been listed and described, as well as a pocket telescope, on the inventory; there is one surveying compass on a Jacob's staff with the initials LAW, which represents the numerous articles associated with his early profession and his continued interest in it and which now is kept in the restored closet. A whip stock, sometimes referred to as a riding crop, is lying on one small table and a bootjack is under the dressing table; neither the whip stock nor the bootjack is an original piece.

Two different styles of windows were used on the north and south ends of the house. The library has two windows of

Georgian design while the banquet room has one large window of Palladian design. The use of two styles was not unusual in that asymmetrical arrangements of windows in the gable ends continued even after a great many of the houses had formalized fronts. The windows in the library have nine panes and movable sashes unlike most Georgian houses which had windows with six panes in a sash. Window glass was considered personal property in England prior to the settlement of America; a person removed his glass from a house and took it to his next residence.[28] A glass tax and fewer windows for security from attack combined to contribute to the smallness of early windows. Therefore, the essential characteristics of the evolution of the window are its size, an increase in the number and size of panes, and the switch from leading to wood muntins to secure the panes. The panes are eight and one-half by ten inches in the library, having one and one-half inch muntins. The six-inch frames on the windows have mitered corners and match the door frames in the room.

The windows in early houses also were placed high enough to permit furniture to be arranged under them. The windows' lower frames and the chair railing are brought together by a board in the library at Mount Vernon. The same line and the color of the ledge of the built-in bookshelves are carried around the room (see Color Plate VII). The molding is the same as that in the downstairs bedroom, which, as part of the older house, reflects colonial taste, while the more ornate molding in the banquet room, finished in 1786, was in the prevailing mode of England (see Illustration 7).

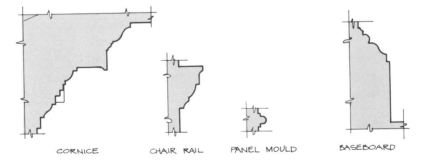

CORNICE   CHAIR RAIL   PANEL MOULD   BASEBOARD

7. Detail drawings of the designs of the wooden paneling, moldings, and decorations in the library.

Shutters may be used inside or outside. The exterior shutters at Mount Vernon now are gray-green, louvered ones and serve as decoration although in the earliest days of the colonies shutters would have been for protection from raids, in which case the shutters could have been solid or paneled. In George Washington's time they might have been used to shut out sun and to cool a south room in Virginia. "*Venetian shutters*" were ordered in November, 1796, for the west side of the house. One shutter on the southeast library window is divided into two equal parts because the roof of the shed prevents its entire length from lying flat against the wall of the house (see Color Plate III).

The dirt, water, or strong light that may be admitted through a window can be a hazard to the books in the collection; therefore, the value of a window is determined by the view without and the drapery within. The sunlight where the window is providing some of the needed light may be controlled or screened by using a combination of a light, sheer, translucent or glass curtain for daytime, and at night a heavy velvet or antique silk drape which can be pulled across for warmth and privacy. Curtains should not obscure but soften the light. Elaborate or patterned drapes or bright solids may destroy the harmony of a room and make the reader conscious of the draperies when studying; draperies may be highlighted in the library which is considered a night room or a Sunday room. Although Washington did not work late at night, it was dark for some of the hours he spent there in the evening and certainly at four o'clock in the morning, chilly as well. Washington wanted a Venetian blind.

To GEORGE AUGUSTINE WASHINGTON
Philadelphia, June 10, 1787
Desire Matthew to give me the exact dimension of the windows [one will do] of the dining room; within the casement [in the room] that I may get a Venetian blind, such as draws up and closes, and expands made here, that others may be made by it, at home, the height from the bottom to top, and width is all that is necessary within the casement.

Modern Venetian blinds *only* are used at the library windows now since the inventory does not make any reference to window coverings in the library. A Venetian blind is listed for the downstairs bedroom, and the window coverings of the other rooms are listed.

Sources of light in the library other than the windows were lamps or candles, rather than a chandelier in the ceiling or candle holders on the walls. The absorption of light by wall surfaces or book bindings is negligible at Mount Vernon. Reading and writing, however, required pools of light, often supplied by Argand sperm-oil lights. The Argand lamp provided more light and was cheaper than candles. George Washington had ordered less costly Argands than those Gouverneur Morris purchased for him in France—fourteen tureen or boat-shaped ones at Ł36.15. The light, either for table or wall, which in 1780 Argand had fitted with a plaited wick in a cylindrical form, had an improved draft which placed less waste in the air.[29] Lamps received daily maintenance, the trimming of wicks and the supplying of fuel; and it is assumed that they were in another part of the house and for that reason the lamps do not appear on the inventory of the library although needed in the library. Four of the Argand lamps are at Mount Vernon, but none are placed in the library now. Instead, a large mobile candle holder of the period has been placed in the room (see Frontispiece). A diarist of the period commented on a room in a home being brilliantly lighted with seven candles.

Covering floors with sand, in some instances sweeping the sand into designs, continued until 1780; but also brick floors, skins, painted canvas or painted designs on wooded floors, and bare floors existed.[30] Probably most common in the eighteenth century was a bare oak or pine wood floor with boards of random widths and thicknesses. Often the first level had a double floor. The original pine wooden boards of the library floor at Mount Vernon seem to have slightly more irregularity of widths than the boards in the older area of the house. The flooring is laid north to south and is not tongue and groove.[31] The upper surfaces and edges of the floor boards were planed and the underside left rough. A black wooden baseboard with molding, measuring altogether approximately seven inches, is used in several rooms including the library (see Illustration 7 and Color Plate VII). Rugs were considered elegant and were much sought by Americans after the Revolution. The French considered the American use of rugs an expression of taste and not a practical concern for warmth.[32] Washington said he would like a *"Wilton if not too much dearer than Scotch"* for the parlor. Later he found that Martha Washington had heard of another type which he called *"Russian"* and sought it. None of the rugs of his time have survived. The rug in the library was removed in the restoration of the library completed in 1975 (see Frontispiece). The absence of a rug *and* drapes robs the room of any color although bright colors, which can be distracting, should be avoided. A room with paneling is considered formal and demands a certain standard of decoration which may be accomplished by the right choice of fabrics for the upholstery. The library at Mount Vernon may seem very austere, for only the brasses and the woods of the furniture produce warmth. The book bindings when kept behind glass can do little to add color.

The east and north walls of the library are mostly wood, painted buff. The other walls are plaster, the color of putty, with only the cornice and chair rail painted buff. "Paint reveals" (areas of a few inches where all previous layers of paint are shown) are on the fireplace and the built-in bookshelves. The restoration color for the woodwork in the study was concluded to be the one found on the bookshelves. It is assumed to have been the color selected by Washington when the bookshelves were installed and to have remained intact for the last eleven or twelve years of his life. (There is an erroneous idea that colonial interiors were always painted a snowy white.[33]) Other colors used were neutrals and were termed: lilac, pearl gray, ashes of roses, mustard, and plum. George Washington ordered for the banquet room buff paint *"of the lightest kind inclining to white."*

As the Georgian period progressed, wall panels became fewer and larger. Wood paneling could be done on the spot while wallpaper had to be ordered from abroad. Washington was believed to have been the first American to order wallpaper, according to an invoice in 1757. The best wallpaper came from China and often was patterned with birds, monkeys, and fruit. Plaster was used for ceilings more often than walls, and wood paneling for walls prevailed through the eighteenth century. It slowly gave way to wallpaper, first above the chair rail and eventually on the entire wall surface. The east entry and stairwell of the library wing were papered; only a small portion of the west entry was papered (see Illustration 5).

The paneling in the library of Mount Vernon follows the shapes created by the existing wall planes and is pleasingly proportioned. Paneling was used in England very early, and a sheathing of wood was used in colonial homes to form the added interior wall, but usually on the fireplace wall first. The paneling, which was good insulation, was often simple tongue and groove, wide, vertically placed. The paneling in the library of Mount Vernon has a sunken molding with a beveled raised panel. The paint does not have a sheen to give color through the reflection of other colors in the room. Dark paneling, waxed, is popular; but its heaviness would not have been as good for Mount Vernon as the choice made.

The paneling on the walls of a home library blends with the shelving, which is generally of wood also. Cupboards and chests had been used extensively for book storage as well as tables, the latter especially for Bibles. The eighteenth century saw the beginning of shelves of rather an elaborate nature. Bookshelves are always better if built-in; the necessary bracing is more adequately provided by the wall structure. They should look built-in, and they should blend with the architectural style of the room.

George Washington was forced to lose a foot of space behind his shelving in order to accomplish a surface flush with the wall of the room (see Illustration 4 and Color Plate VII). If placed on the west wall the case might have afforded sound-proofing where most needed; the one-foot air space on the east wall did this although it was not needed unless the stairway was used by a considerable number of people. Much use of the stairs was highly unlikely since the area was restricted. The second floor bedroom above the library was used by Martha and

George Washington and had entry only by the stairway from the first floor library wing in their lifetime. The ceiling did not provide soundproofing from footsteps above, but the presence in the room of Mrs. Washington or a servant would not be assumed to be excessive or have coincided with Washington's schedule in the library.

The design of the glass doors of the bookshelves does not repeat a design used elsewhere in the room, such as over a door or a window or in the desk or breakfront. The arches suggest the roundness expressed in the pattern seen on the mantel of the fireplace and in the doors of the desk. The shelving was placed on Friday, June 16, 1786, as his diary notes: *"Began about 10 Oclock to put up the Book press in my study."* The word press meant a place for storage, not a copying device. Only the two shelves at the top were found to be fixed. The book press ceilings had grooves which coincided with grooves found in the fixed shelves below, indicating that partitions had once made compartments for ledgers and documents. These compartments have been replaced (see Color Plate VIII). These partitioned areas formed a filing area close at hand in the manner of the period for cash memorandum books and personal correspondence.

> *Confident I am that there is no authentic document relative to your Land among my Papers at Mount Vernon—but as I surveyed most of the Lands about Bullskin, it is possible, tho' not at all probable, some minutes may be found or rough draughts had of these lands among my Papers which might lead to some discovery more important; and, if any exist, they are to be found in my Study, among my Land Papers in small parchment covered Books tied together; or in a broad untied bundle of loose & old Plats of Surveys in the Pidgeon holes which are labelled Land Papers.*

The shelves were unpainted in their first state of use and appear now as they did originally. In a small library too few shelves are better than too many, but space should be allowed for future growth. The book press at Mount Vernon is seven feet tall, eighteen inches deep, each of the four banks twenty-five inches wide. They provide approximately thirty-six feet of shelf space. The shelf is of five-eighth inch pine wood and the shelves are not warped. Glass fronts protect books from dust and are more sanitary but leave the books less accessible. Books, if not placed in covered shelving, are more inviting and lend their color to the room, often picking up the prevailing colors in the rug, not the drapes. Glass is not easily broken in slamming the doors since air in the case acts as a cushion; however, a few of the panes are broken at Mount Vernon. Each pane is eleven inches wide and twleve and one-half inches in height. Each door has three hinges and two locks, probably due to the slenderness and fragility of the door. The volumes housed in the press are a mixture of authentic titles and duplicates of original titles. The letters are "dummies."

The top shelves are often designed for special pieces of sculpture or other art objects. The top shelf for books should be no more than five feet from the floor. Titles cannot be read or books secured from the shelves if the shelves are too high, but Washington was over six feet tall and seemed to prefer the higher shelves for items he consulted as often as he did the books on the middle shelves. He could also use the bottom shelf of the cupboard below the press as a step. Washington seemed not to have employed any form of library steps or any of the ingenious devices for reaching the higher shelves such as Franklin's calipers on a pole for forking down books or Jefferson's folding ladder-table.

Cupboards were built into the lower half of the shelving and utilized for storage (see Color Plate VII). The two-shelved cabinets at Mount Vernon may have been used for maps or newspapers. Manuscripts, still fairly common at that time as an inheritance in English home libraries, may have dictated including cabinets which would permit placing a volume flat on a shelf. The design of the press may have followed the English example. The Trumbull prints, probably of military scenes, which are listed on the inventory or the twenty other prints attributed to the room in the inventory of 1800 may have been inside the cabinets at one time. The prints are represented now by two portfolios leaning against the cabinets. A projection or ledge of sufficient width, above the cabinets and below the shelving, on which to rest a book, was not included at Mount Vernon. The ledge is only one inch in width, thirty-six inches from the floor.

Fixed shelving will not destroy symmetry of line but must be designed for a variety of heights of books. The bookshelves at Mount Vernon are adjustable every three inches, with the exception of the bottom shelf, which cannot be adjusted to less than nine inches. The shelves are sufficiently deep to have made the shelving of another row of books behind the front row of books quite easy, a common practice of the time.

Chapter III

Furniture in the
Library of Mount Vernon

Many of the homes in America in the eighteenth century were gracious and livable and the furnishings, pleasing. The furniture was attractive, trim, and practical, beginning to be more formal but not yet classic. Wood was always plentiful for construction of furniture needed in the colonies and few possessions had been brought from Europe by the colonists. Much of the furniture was homemade and utilitarian with the earlier pieces being made for the kitchen. John Alden was probably the first cabinet or furniture maker. As the country developed, cabinetmakers opened shops in the cities and by the beginning of the eighteenth century was turning out high-backed chairs, gate-leg tables, desks, bookcases, and other pieces of furniture in oak, pine, cherry, maple, or walnut. Designs from England were copied, but some distinctly American pieces, such as the highboy and the Windsor chair, were developed. Mahogany, imported from San Domingo, was used for the Chippendale designs that were in style just prior to the Revolution.

The American-born aristocrat usually considered his education incomplete until he had visited the mother country, where he usually acquired a taste for the newest and most fashionable furniture and the idea of establishing a beautiful house at home.[1] Thomas Jefferson sent back eighty-six cases of furnishings from France.[2] George Washington, although he did not travel to Europe, was conscious of the styles and qualities of furniture as well as being interested in architecture and land-scaping.

Washington's early purchase in January, 1755, of six chairs with leather seats from a fellow officer is well documented, as are his other almost annual purchases of chairs, tables, and beds from abroad.[3] However, he was cognizant of the risks of imports, writing:

This a custom, I have some Reason to believe, with many shop keepers, and Tradesmen in London when they know the Goods are bespoke for Exportation to palm sometimes old, and sometimes very slight and Indifferent Goods upon Us taking care at the same time to advance 10, 15, or perhaps 20 pr Ct. upon them.

Washington bought locally as well. When George William Fairfax and his wife, Sally Cary Fairfax, Washington's neighbors at Belvoir, returned to England, he disposed of their beautiful household furnishings for them by having a sale in the summer of 1774, buying several items himself. Not until 1783, when the war ended, however, was Washington once again able to buy furniture for Mount Vernon. From camp at Rocky Hill, New Jersey, he wrote to his nephew Bushrod Washington, then studying law in Philadelphia:

Let me beg of you to make enquiry of some of the best Cabinet makers, at what price, and in what time, two dozen strong, neat and plain, but fashionable, Table chairs [I mean chairs for a dining room] could be had; with strong canvas bottoms to receive a loose covering of check, or worsted, as I may hereafter choose.

Next, the General wrote to Robert Morris, the Superintendent of Finance, asking him to furnish Mrs. Washington with $1500. He explained that since she was on her way home from camp, *"it would be very convenient for me, that she should procure at Philadelphia some Articles of Furniture and stores for my House in Virginia."*

Before he arrived to take up residency in Philadelphia, Washington worried about the rooms being hung with tapestry or rich and costly paper, neither of which would suit his furniture,[4] which was not beyond that found in the homes of wealthy Americans generally and might have been called plain. The dressing table, which was kept in the library during his lifetime, was bought from a group of pieces sold by the retiring French minister, Comte de Moustier, whose house it was that he inhabited in New York at the beginning of his presidency. The dressing table, twenty-nine inches high, thirty-eight inches wide, and twenty-five inches deep, is mahogany with European white fir as the secondary wood. The wooden top is hinged and opens to show the inset mirror and marble table surface. The original drawer pulls are missing (see Illustration 6 in Chapter II). Using the dressing table for shaving, sitting or standing, seems enormously uncomfortable.

From the collection of household goods, Washington sent ninety-seven boxes, fourteen trunks, forty-three casks, thirteen packages, and three hampers by sloop to Mount Vernon when he retired from the presidency. There was an inventory made when he moved from Philadelphia of private and public possessions, the latter referring to government property. There is a good deal of evidence through the many letters to his secretary, Tobias Lear, some sent from the overnight stops on the trip to Mount Vernon after retirement from office, that moving back to Mount Vernon was uppermost in his mind at this time. Yet, at Mount Vernon

> . . . in a word, I am already surrounded by joiners, masons, and painters; and such is my anxiety to get out of their hands, that I have scarcely a room to put a friend into or to sit in myself, without the music of hammers or the odoriferous scent of paint.

It is from this time that the furniture of the library of Mount Vernon was recorded.

Inventories of household furnishings were fairly prevalent in the colonies, having served other purposes besides the settlement of an estate upon the death of the owner. Englishmen, returning home with financial loss, inventoried possessions for possible claims against the Crown. Unfortunately, inventories are not usually written with sufficient descriptions of such items as tables and chairs to afford much help in identification, but the inventory of the library at Mount Vernon has been a source for the restoration work of the furnishings in keeping with the library's original purpose (see Appendix I). The chairs and tables, with the exception of the breakfast table, are period pieces.

The furniture kept in the library since the first restoration of it in 1929 has always included the tambour desk and the revolving chair, the terrestrial globe, the iron chest, and a bust of Washington by Houdon, all items known to have been in the library during Washington's lifetime. The globe and the bust have never left the library. Among the other interesting objects listed on the study or library inventory and kept in the museum at Mount Vernon are some of the numerous pistols, swords, spye glasses, surveying instruments, dentist's instruments, and a telescope. The swords were willed by Washington in the following manner:

> To each of my nephews Augustine, George Lewis, George Steptoe, Bushrod, and Samuel I give one of my swords or cutteaux of which I may die possessed and they are to chuse in the order they are named: These swords are accompanied with an injunction not to unsheath them for the purpose of shedding blood, except it be for self-defence or in the defence of their country and its rights; and in the latter case, to keep them unsheathed and prefer falling with them in their hands, to the relinquishment thereof.

Three of the five swords are on display in the museum; his eye glasses and case are also kept in the museum. Eyeglasses of the period are shown lying on a table in the library on copies of *The Spectator*, November 28, 1798, and *The Gazette of the United States*, April 23, 1791.

Probably the most important item of furnishing in a library is either an easy chair or rocker in which to read in a relaxing position or the desk and chair which suit the work routine of the owner. The library did not have sufficient space for a large table *and* a sofa. There seems to be no evidence of a sofa ever having been in the library. Neither is there a library table. The English used this term for any flat top desk which the Americans called a pedestal or a kneehole desk. Library tables, as designed by Chippendale, were generally large and double-pedestal tables with drawers and often a space for books.

The room could provide for an easy chair as well as the two other large pieces of furniture, the tambour desk and the breakfront secretary-bookcase. An easy chair, or French chair as it was sometimes known, has been in the library (see Color Plate VII) but has a lack of provenance and has been known as one of the "supposed's." The covered wing chair, supposedly Mary Ball Washington's, was placed in the library in 1953 and remained there until the 1975 restoration of the library. Money was raised in 1910 to purchase the leather-covered armchair which was already on loan to Mount Vernon. Supposed to have belonged to George Washington's mother when he was an infant, its presence there during his lifetime is very unlikely, and there is no record of his mother having visited the house after 1752. Washington did not own the chair but probably used it in 1775 at his headquarters in Craigie House, the Long-fellow House in Cambridge, Massachusetts. The armchair, was recovered in chintz when placed in the bedroom and its covering changed to damask when it was moved to the library. The fabric chosen for covering the chair was similar to the textiles, as many as forty varieties, advertised in colonial newspapers.[5] Upholstering a chair, with the exception of the legs, had been introduced in the early eighteenth century in the period of William and Mary, the advantage of an upholstered wing chair being protection from drafts.

The library of Mount Vernon has a minimum number of chairs. The three side chairs placed in the library are of Chippendale design. Georgian architecture was complimented by Chippendale furniture in the middle of the eighteenth century. More and more people chose furniture which was well-constructed and designed in good taste. This was especially true after the publication of a book of designs, *The Gentleman and the Cabinetmaker's Directory*, by Chippendale. Published in 1754, it ran to three editions. The originals of Chippendale brought high prices, but many pieces from local shops carried the designs. The side chairs in the library at Mount Vernon have pierced splats of delicate scale; the legs are cabriole, at-trributed to the Queen Anne period; and the seats are covered

in black horsehair. The simple carving and open work for ornamentation, to which mahogany lent itself, were characteristics
of the Chippendale period. A fourth chair in the library has a
moulded leaf design on the knee. The moulded leaf design used
by American cabinetmakers who had clustered in Philadelphia
was unknown to the English manufacturers who used the shell
and acanthus leaf.[6] The ball and claw foot was used in America
with Chippendale designs although not shown in his book or
used in England. Pride in local crafts which were of a quality to
warrant esteem and the anti-English sentiment lessened the
amount of imports of furniture. The chairs were probably all
made in Philadelphia and similar ones were in the homes of
other prominent people, such as that of Samuel Powel in
Philadelphia, in whose home George and Martha Washington
celebrated their twentieth wedding anniversary. A Queen Anne
arm chair now in the library has graceful slipper feet, uniquely
curved arms and a single splat in the back topped with a carved
shell. Any of the chairs could have been used, comfortably,
at one of the small tables for writing or as an extra chair for
guests. However, the inventory lists only two chairs, an arm
chair and a circular chair, Washington's desk chair. One may
speculate that his secretaries or farm managers did not sit while
there and that guests whom Washington invited to the library
had to wait until a servant could bring more chairs.

One of the most baffling references in records related to
Mount Vernon furniture is to a chair which is described in the
inventory as a *"Fan Chair,"* which may be the one listed in the
inventory in the appendix as an arm chair. This was listed as
being in Washington's study and had been purchased by him in
Philadelphia in August, 1787, while attending the Constitutional Convention. His *Cash Memorandum Book* records a
payment of £1.12.6 for a fan chair, which Clement Biddle, his
agent, was later asked to forward to Mount Vernon. In the
draft copy of the inventory of Martha Washington's estate
there is listed in the lumber room a *"Chear wt. Fan,"* amended
in the second copy of this inventory to *"Fan Chair."* It was
purchased by John Mason for $7 at the July, 1802 sale of fur-
nishings of Mrs. Washington's estate and has since dropped out
of sight. This chair may have been, as suggested by Marion Day

Iverson in her book *The American Chair*, a copy of Benjamin Franklin's fan chair. This was described, by a contemporary of Franklin, as a chair with rockers and a large fan placed over it, with which he cooled himself and kept off flies while he sat reading, with only a small motion of his foot. Certainly, if Washington's fan chair was like Franklin's, it would have been a useful if not attractive appendage of the General's study. One can only sympathize with Mrs. Washington for moving it to the lumber room after his death. It has not been returned to Mount Vernon.

The two tables in the room are well chosen for the proportions of the room. Small tables abounded for the many activities of households; particularly, however, were they necessary for lights. Card tables were also plentiful; they had a flat top and appeared on colonial inventories as early as 1727. Southern-made card table had five legs, four stationary and the fifth swinging out to support the top when open.[7] One card table in the Mount Vernon library has but three legs stationary and the fourth swinging (see Color Plate VII); therefore, it is questionable that it is of Southern make. Chippendale used two types of legs, the cabriole and a square, perfectly straight leg of the same size from top to bottom with a slight chamfer or oblique cut on the inner edge.[8] The table in the library is mahogany Chippendale, circa 1770-1800; the secondary wood is pitch pine. Its dimensions are twenty-eight and one-fourth inches high, thirty-three inches wide, fifteen and one-half inches in depth, and when open, thirty-one inches in depth; the brasses are replacements.

It is interesting to note that in Washington's account books there are frequent entries of winnings and losings without any apparent thought of the right or wrong of gambling.[9] In his diary is an entry *"at home all day over cards."* He liked cards, bought cards by the dozen packs at a time, and ordered card tables in pairs. Games of chance offered great diversion to a company with sporting proclivities. A loo table at Mount Vernon in the west parlor has both felt-lined corners for candlesticks and oval depressions known as "fish ponds" where small mother-of-pearl loo counters, carved in the form of fishes, were kept.

The inventory listed one walnut and two pine tables. In the restoration of the library in 1975 the black walnut wedding breakfast table was placed in the library and one of the card tables was removed. The small stretchered table, on which George and Martha Washington ate their wedding breakfast at the home of the bride, a tradition in her family, is obviously country-made (see Illustration 1). Seventeenth-century furniture was constructed of solid wood, with only a rubbed finish and little or no metal employed. Its rectangular paneled construction gave way to the curve in the eighteenth century, and after the Revolution the influence of Hepplewhite and Sheraton was felt.

1. Breakfast Table. Black walnut; American, probably southern, ca. 1759. H: 28"; W: 31½"; D:25".

The slant top desk had its origin in the simple Bible box, and the design has persisted in portable desks and school desks until the present day. As the box increased in size to fit the top of a table, the uprights or legs gave way to a chest of drawers under the top. At the height of the Chippendale era, compartments and small drawers were introduced inside the enclosed desk area. It was the golden age of letter writing and diary-keeping; the desk was essential. In the second quarter of the eighteenth century the secretary-desk in one piece came into existence. It took its name from the French word *escritoire*[10] and had a bookcase above the desk. This bookcase could have wooden, mirror, or glass doors; but a common design in the colonies employed thirteen glass panes in each door in a variety of designs (see Color Plate IX).

The tambour-front secretary was introduced late in the eighteenth century by Hepplewhite. A tambour front combined flexible or finely reeded woodwork and a canvas or heavy linen cloth into a door to cover or close the desk area. Veneers of rosewood, apple, tulip, or satin wood, to produce a richness of surface and variety of color, were used. Some of these woods were imported. In 1791, a report given by Alexander Hamilton, Secretary of the Treasury, to the House of Representatives on the subject of manufactures states

> cabinet-wares are generally made little, if at all inferior to those of Europe. Their extent is such as to have admitted of considerable exportation. An exemption from duty of the several kinds of wood ordinarily used in these manufactures seems to be all that is requisite by way of encouragement.[11]

Before leaving Philadelphia the retiring President paid John Aitken $145 for a *"tambour Secretary and book case."* This piece of furniture, made in 1797, is one of the best documented of all of the original furnishings now at Mount Vernon. The design is by Hepplewhite. The primary wood is mahogany and the secondary woods are yellow poplar and white pine; its dimensions are ninety-five and three-fourth inches high, thirty-eight inches wide, and twenty-eight inches deep. The desk has glass doors with thirteen panes and the hardware of the Hepplewhite period. It has been shown with and without the brass eagle finial and in an earlier period with curtains on the doors.

The curve of the kneehole is repeated in the reverse curves of the pediment at the top. There is a well (flush sliding panel in the writing surface) but no secret drawers. The width of the kneehole is only fifteen inches. George Washington would have been uncomfortable at the desk without the sliding surface upon which to write and the lowered, leather chair whose legs were shortened for him. It was in this desk supposedly that the wills were kept. Washington sent Mrs. Washington at 4:30 A.M., as he approached his death, down to *"his room"* (the library) to bring him the wills. He selected one as worthless and requested her to burn it, which she did. Today only one desk is kept there despite the listing of another desk and two pine writing tables on the inventory.

The desk was bequeathed by Washington to Dr. James Craik with the following words, *"To my compatriot in arms, and old & intimate friend Doctr. Craik, I give my Bureau [or as the Cabinet makers call it, Tambour Secretary,"* which with the circular desk chair, was *"an appendage of my Study."* This piece of furniture was a treasured possession of the descendants of Dr. Craik until 1905 when it was purchased by the Association from his heirs in Kentucky and returned to Washington's study.

With the desk was the *"Uncommon Chair."* President Washington patronized the shop of Thomas Burling, cabinet-maker, 36 Beekman Street in New York, and purchased a number of articles of furniture. The "Uncom^n and Ch^r," for which Burling was paid Ł7 in April 1790, is easily identified as General Washington's desk chair. It appears on the list of household furniture compiled by President Washington before his retirement and again in the inventory of his estate, both times listed as a "Circular Chair." It was specified in his will as *"the circular chair"* and devised along with his secretary-desk to Dr. James Craik, who had served with him through the French and Indian and Revolutionary Wars. Craik was one of the physicians in attendance at his last illness. The chair was returned to Mount Vernon from the heirs of Andrew Jackson. Its distinctive feature, revolving or swiveling, is provided by wooden rollers, some of which have had to be replaced (see Color Plate IX).

Among the rarest pieces of antique furniture are book-cases. There were secretaries; but apart from these, evidently few people in colonial days had books enough to warrant commissioning a cabinetmaker to build bookcases for them,[12] or they used built-in shelves constructed for their books. However, Josiah Claypoole advertised desks and bookcases in 1740 as made in his shop.[13] In Chippendale's book of designs a number of examples of bookcases are shown, but it was not until the Sheraton influence was in full force that many book-cases, which were costly, were produced in America. They were usually produced on special order for the dimensions of a particular location.

The bookcase which Washington had his personal friend and agent, Colonel Clement Biddle, buy for him in 1798 is represented at Mount Vernon now by a breakfront secretary-bookcase whose top center drawer opens to make a desk (see Illustration 2). On January 1, 1799, Tobias Lear, his secretary, wrote to speed the delivery of the piece from the shop of John Douglass in Philadelphia which had been purchased for $133.33, was shipped crated for an additional $18.80, and arrived in February, 1799, on board the *Harmony*. This was over ten years after Washington had installed the built-in shelving and only a short time before his death. Probably the last piece of furniture purchased by Washington for Mount Vernon, it was described as *"A liberry Bookcase"* during purchase but is not listed on the inventory, list of sales, or in the will in that manner. The original was inherited by Henry L. Daingerfield Lewis from his grandmother Nelly Custis Lewis and identified by him as a Mount Vernon piece. It is not likely that the one there now is the original. The breakfront secretary-bookcase was quite common, having been designed by Chippendale, Hepplewhite, and Sheraton with many variations of doors, drawers, and shelves. Some had a drawer above the writing area as well as below if they were extremely tall. Some were only two doors wide, others four, extending to nine feet in width. A few had only two drawers placed near the floor and a

2. Breakfront Secretary-Bookcase. Sheraton. Mahogany; secondary wood, white pine. American, Salem, ca. 1790-1800. The brass ornaments on top are replacements. H: 6'9 1/2''; W: 5'7 3/8''; D: 19 3/4''.

COLOR PLATES

I. View of Mount Vernon from the west showing the beveled boards in imitation of stone.

II. A view of the central hall looking to the East through the west entry with its classic pillars and pediment which are repeated inside.

III. The Mansion House, east front, showing piazza, the library wing, and the south colonnade. A small shed covers the steps to the cellar. Shutter on window nearest the shed has been divided to permit the top, right half to lie flat against the house.

IV. Library Mantel, showing carving and paneling, as well as accessories representative of the colonial period of home decoration. The English horn for hunting is an authentic Mount Vernon piece.

V. Fireplace placed by Washington in the banquet room, the gift of Samuel Vaughan, a wealthy London merchant, from his library in Wanstead, England.

VI. Southern view of estate and Potomac River that can be seen from library windows.

VII. Library showing the built-in bookshelves (book press) on east wall. Photo taken before the restoration completed in 1975 when the rug and the drapes were removed.

VIII. Upper section of book press, showing restored sections for filing papers.

IX. The library, Mount Vernon west wall. Photo taken before the restoration completed in 1975.

X. Houdon bust of George Washington, 1785.

XI. The dimensions of the iron chest are 20 1/2 x 12 3/4 x 11 1/2 inches. The key has been lost.

XII. Washington's brass telescope.

XIII. Washington gave 2 volumes of **Botanical Magazine** to his stepgranddaughter, Nelly Custis.

greater number of shelves for storage, making them resemble a china closet, which purpose they often served.

The library room in Mount Vernon afforded no space for a built-in corner cupboard, which had come into use in 1710. These cabinets, sometimes movable pieces after 1750,[14] often had fine workmanship and woods, employing the shell or sunburst design at the top and inlay or tracery on the fronts. They ususally coordinated with the architectural features of the room but provided little space for books and were better for dishes or statuary.

If all the pieces attributed to the library by the inventory were placed in the room, certainly a more crowded, less desirable appearance would probably result, according to today's standards for furniture arrangement. However, the major pieces of furniture have been there and arranged in much the same manner for many years, primarily due to the fixed location of the book press and the fireplace. Small items from time to time have been shifted or removed. An incidence of the latter is a glass tumbler which no longer appears on the writing surface of the tambour desk. The fact that a tumbler appeared marked out on one copy of the inventory may be the reason it no longer is there, or the homey touch created by the glass may have been achieved by returning the dressing table to the library.

The large terrestrial globe had been made at Washington's request in London, delivered to him in New York, and must have traveled with him to Philadelphia during the first year of his presidency and thence to his study at Mount Vernon on his final homecoming in 1797 (see Color Plate VII). The globe was not removed from the house when the last Washington left, having a continuous history of residence at Mount Vernon. It was presented to the Association in 1858 by the last private owner, Colonel John A. Washington, Jr.

In the summer of 1789, President Washington had inquired about purchasing a terrestrial globe from England through Messrs. Wakelin Welch & Sons, a firm of London business agents. They replied to his inquiry in October, as follows:

> One Adams here is suppos'd to be the first Optician
> we have, he purposes to make the Terrestrial Globe

upon the New & Approv'd method, it may take up two Months to Compleat & that will be as early as a Conveyance may offer, for after this Vessell, none is expected to Sail before Febry.

According to the original bill, dated February 10, 1790, a twenty-eight inch terrestrial globe was purchased from George Adams, Mathematical Instrument Maker, To his Majesty, At Tycho Brahe's Head, No. 60 Fleet Street. The total cost, including two scientific books and packing charges, amounted to £27.12.6. The globe is listed on the inventory of Mrs. Washington's estate. After Washington's death it remained at Mount Vernon with the books in the library which had been bequeathed to Judge Bushrod Washington. The original stretchers and brass support are now missing. The globe rests on a mahogany Hepplewhite stand, thirty-four inches high, thirty-five and three-eighth inches in diameter.

The Houdon bust of Washington is the "most treasured object in the Mount Vernon collection" and is kept in the museum[15] (see Color Plate X). A copy of the bust by Clark Mills made prior to 1859 is now in the library. Franklin and Jefferson engaged Jean Antoine Houdon, a portrait sculptor, then without a rival in the world, to go to America from Paris for the purpose of making a statue of Washington for the rotunda of the capitol of Virginia at Richmond. The terms were 25,000 livres (about $4,620) for the statue and pedestal. They agreed to pay his expenses and to pay his family 10,000 livres in case he died enroute. To insure the state of Virginia against loss, they procured insurance upon Houdon's life. Houdon came to the United States on the same boat with Franklin. On September 20, 1785, he gave Houdon a letter of introduction to Washington and also wrote to Washington to apprise him of the sculptor's arrival. Washington wrote to Houdon that he was welcome, also asking if there was anything he could procure that was necessary to Houdon's purpose.[16] On Sunday, October 2, 1785,

after we were in Bed [about eleven Oclock in the Evening] Mr. Houdon and three young men assistants arrived at Mount Vernon by Water from Alexandria, introduced by a Mr. Perin, a French Gentleman of Alexandria

who may have been acting as interpreter. Washington sat for two successive days for the sculptor.

For three days the artist had kept his subject under close observation, seeking the pose he would perpetuate. Finally, according to an anecdote reported in a Philadelphia newspaper a century ago, he was invited to join the General in viewing a span of horses offered by a dealer. The asking price, the account relates, "so moved Washington's indignation, that he bade the fellow begone." It was this moment of disdainful rejection which the sculptor chose to depict.[17]

The bust was lightly fired, probably in the oven of the family kitchen. The result was probably imperfect but the best obtainable under the circumstances; without this treatment the bust could scarcely have survived. This clay model was left at Mount Vernon and placed above the door of the library by George Washington's own hands. It was whitewashed to resemble marble or plaster of Paris. This original clay bust of George Washington was bought at public auction by Bushrod Washington, and it has never left Mount Vernon, having been given to the Association by the last private owner of Mount Vernon.

Houdon's bust possesses unique virtue as a three-dimensional likeness of Washington, done in the prime of his life by one of the greatest sculptors of his age. It affords a standard of fidelity by which the multiplicity of other portraits may be judged. That this belief reflects the opinion of Washington's contemporaries is indicated by a statement of John A. Washington, Jr., who wrote,

> It may not be amiss for me to add that Major and Mrs. Lawrence Lewis have repeatedly told me that they thought Houdon's bust here the best representation of Gen. Washington's face they had ever seen and I know that the late Judge Bushrod Washington was of the same opinion. These persons were not only familiar with Gen. Washington's face but had ample opportunities during his life of comparing it with the bust.[18]

For the full-length statue Houdon took exact measurements of the person of Washington and ample notes on costume before he left to return to Paris, having spent a fortnight at Mount Vernon. The statue of Italian marble was not finished until 1789. It is believed that Houdon also took a life mask of Washington, as authenticated by the following letter in 1849 of Eleanor Parke Lewis, better known by her unmarried name, Nelly Custis.

> I was only six years old at that time, and perhaps should not have retained any recollection of Houdon & his visit, had I not seen the General as I supposed, dead, & laid out on a large table cover'd with a sheet. I was passing the white servants Hall & saw as I thought the Corpse of one I consider'd my Father, I went in, & found the General extended on his back on a large table, a sheet over him, except his face, on which Houdon was engaged in putting on plaster to form the cast. Quills were in his nostrils. I was very much alarmed until I was told that it was a bust, a likeness of the General, & would not injure him. This is all I recollect.[19]

It is also believed that Houdon took the life mask personally to Paris, and a positive plaster cast of the clay bust was taken separately by his workmen.

Also in the inventory, listed as a bust in plaster, was one of John Paul Jones by Houdon, valued at $20. The one now in the library is a modern copy done in 1945. The original was burned in a fire at the Washington Lodge in Alexandria. John Paul Jones liked the original and had five made, one of which was a gift from him to Washington.

Washington placed the little bust of Necker upon a bracket over the fireplace in the library himself in the autumn of 1790. Through an exchange agreement with the Historical Society of Pennsylvania, the Sèvres bust of Jacques Necker, the French minister of finance, has been restored to the library. Not only were busts one means of communication about heroes of the day, but also Washington seemed to like statuary of military heroes. In 1759, when he did not receive the ones ordered, he refused to accept philosophers and poets as substitutes:

Directions for the Busts:
4. One of Alexander the Great; another of Julius
Caesar; another of Charles XII. of Sweden; and a
fourth of the King of Prussia. N.B. These are not to
exceed fifteen inches in height, nor ten in width.
2 Other busts, of Prince Eugene and the Duke of
Marlborough, somewhat smaller.

Busts were known to be popular decorations for the top shelves of libraries and presented one form of art for the home, but Washington did not have shelving suitable for busts. Brackets have been installed over each of the three doors which can accommodate them and upon the brackets are placed the busts of Washington (southwest door), Jones (west door), and Necker (east door). The bracket over the fireplace has been removed.

Also on the inventory was a profile in plaster of Washington by Joseph Wright. *"A better likeness of me than any other painter has done,"* said George Washington of the oil by Wright, which seemed to give *"the distinguishing characteristics with more boldness than delicacy."* It was one of eleven likenesses of Washington in Mount Vernon at the time of his death. Of the profile in plaster he said nothing and put it in the library (see Color Plate IX). In the profile-portrait Washington was given the attribute of a leader of ancient times with a garland upon his head. In his memoirs, Elkanah Watson gives a long account of Wright, the painter and artist of some eminence, who in 1784 took a model of Washington's head in plaster:

I heard from Washington himself, an amusing anecdote connected with the bust. In January, 1785, I enjoyed the inestimable privilege of a visit under his roof, in the absence of all visitors. Among the many interesting subjects which engaged our conversation in a long winter evening, [the most valuable in my life] in which his dignified lady and Miss Custis united, he amused us with relating the incident of the taking of this model. Wright came to Mount Vernon, the General remarked, with the singular request, that I should permit him to take a model of my face, in plaster of Paris, to which I consented, with some reluctance. He oiled my features over; and, placing me flat upon my back, upon a cot, proceeded to daub my face with the plaster. Whilst in this ludicrous attitude, Mrs. Washington entered the room; and seeing my face thus overspread with the plaster, involuntarily exclaimed. Her cry excited in me a disposition to smile, which gave my mouth a slight twist, or compression of the lips, that is now observable in the busts which Wright afterwards made. These are nearly the words of Washington.[20]

It is believed, however, that Wright dropped the mask and that it broke.

Part of the dowry the young widow Custis brought with her when she married George Washington was her late husband's iron treasure chest. For the next forty years Daniel Parke Custis' iron chest was a familiar sight at Mount Vernon where Washington used it for storing his valuables (see Color Plate XI). In May, 1775, before he left for Philadelphia to attend the Second Continental Congress, Washington recorded in his *Cash Memorandum Book* the amount of cash left with Lund, the amount of cash he carried with him, and a small amount of silver and paper currency *"left in my Iron Chest."* There is not any documentation to show that it was bolted to the floor in his time, and it is not bolted now. Also, the floor gives no indication of the bolting; however, the stories of bolting persist. Bolting the chest to the floor seems debatable if it contained valuables since it would have been one of the first items to be removed in case of an emergency. It is under the wedding breakfast table currently. (see Appendix I). The iron chest remained at Mount Vernon in Mrs. Washington's possession until her death in 1802. In her will she bequeathed it to George Washington Parke Custis, who took it to his seat, Arlington House, with his other family pieces. The chest was returned in 1954.

The only one of George Washington's early surveying instruments mentioned in his will was a small telescope in the library. He left it to Dr. David Stuart, a warm friend of his who had married John Parke Custis' widow. Washington also gave the dressing table to him. The telescope is by Whitford of London. The telescope which Lossing sketched[21] is almost identical to the one at Mount Vernon now with the exception of a reversal in the attachment of the legs to the base. It was acquired in 1946 (see Color Plate XII).

The manufacture of paper was forbidden in the colonies by England, and paper was difficult to obtain during the Revolutionary War. Not until about the second year of Washington's presidency did the new industry become a stable supplier.[22] He instructed his manager in 1794 to use *"back of a letter, a piece of waste paper, or slate."* Whether this referred to thriftiness or recall of information as a desirable trait is not known. A ream of paper cost from three to five dollars at that time and was inventoried because of its value. Washington had approximately twenty-five reams on hand in the library, perhaps stored in the four cupboards on either side of the fireplace. The two molds for making the Washington watermark in the paper were also listed in the inventory (see Illustration 3).

Only early rising and concentration alone in the library could have provided the time to keep up with the correspondence. Letters, to and from; invoices, receipts, leases; journals and diaries; addresses and drafts of them; account books and ledgers, memoranda of all sorts; surveys and maps; weekly reports of managers; records of experiments; weather reports; orderly books and orders of the war were all accumulating at Mount Vernon. The recesses on either side of the fireplace and the storage area under the stairway did not provide enough space. In 1797 Washington wrote to James McHenry, Secretary of War, of his intention to erect a special building (the first presidential library) for his military, civil, and private papers, but it never materialized. The bulkiness of paper was cut slightly by the custom of folding and sealing the letter for mailing and not using an envelope. In filing, letters were docketed or labeled with the name of the writer and date and occasionally the subject. Wax was used for sealing letters. Two ivory-handled seals were listed on the inventory. One is described as an engraved steel seal with a large and quaint ivory handle, bearing the coat of arms of the Washington family.

3. General Washington's Watermark, consisting of his name in a circle surrounding a figure of Liberty with pileus and cap and surmounted by the Washington crest, a raven, with wings indorsed, proper, issuing out of a ducal coronet.

Although steel-point pens were available by 1780,[23] and Lossing describes a silver pencase in which was a sliding tube for a common black-lead pencil,[24] (pencil referred to the lead part; later wood was put around it), Washington preferred quills. He cut them himself, seemingly with a never-varying cutting method since the resultant writing stroke was even. A pen knife, which got its name from its use for pointing quill pens, was also used for erasures. In 1799 he lost a favorite pen knife and sought to buy one with two blades. Speculation is that the lost one was given to him by his mother.

He chose ink with care and mixed the powder and water himself. Cakes of ink were in use in 1773, and ink was available bottled by 1790. He ordered a tape, a kind of narrow ribbon, to stitch several sheets of long letters or documents together, tying the ends.[25] On his desk now are a silver ink stand with candle and quills, a pounce box, and sealing wax, which he preferred to wax wafers. The pounce was finely powdered cuttle fish or pumice powder which was used for blotting ink. The excess pounce was poured back into the saucer-shaped rim and through the sprinkler holes into the box for reuse. All these pieces, with the exception of the quills, are authentic Mount Vernon pieces (see Color Plate IX).

A press for copying letters was invented by James Watt of steam engine fame and patented by him in England in 1780. The process for copying involved dampening the press, with slightly sugared water to give adherence, and a coarse-textured tissue paper made especially for the purpose. It was necessary to read the copy "through the tissue." By means of a copying press, Washington kept a record of his official correspondence and the most important of his personal business letters and was doubtless one of the earliest American users of this method of duplication for file purposes. Washington wrote Commodore Alexander Gillon:

Head Quarters, June 17, 1782
I have received by the post your two favors of the 4th March and 6th of June. I feel myself much obliged to you for the Care and Attention you have paid to the two Boxes sent on Board your Ship at Amsterdam;

they contain a Press for Copying Letters, and were
ordered on Board by Messrs De Neufville and Sons,
and designed as a present from them to me. If you will
be pleased to deliver the Boxes to the Order of the
Sectry at War, who will take charge of their forwardg
to me, it will add to the Obligation I am already under
to your Care.

The press was afterwards used at Mount Vernon and appears to
have been taken to New York and Philadelphia for official use
there.

The copying press first enumerated by the executors was
undoubtedly a model purchased by Washington in 1797 from
Joseph Anthony, Philadelphia merchant. This press appears to
have been a more ambitious machine with brass rollers and
springs that were frequently out of adjustment. In fact, we get
the impression that Washington preferred the older copying
machine. In the fall of 1797, just after repairs had been made the
previous month, Washington wrote to Timothy Pickering who
had supervised the work:

The Copying Press came safe, but does not work well;
whether for want of more Springs I am unable to
determine. Having a small one [which used to be
getting out of order frequently, but at present does
tolerably well] I do not use it at all. Should the small
one fail, I will send you the other, and ask you to have
its defects rectified.

Present whereabouts of Washington's letter press-copying
machines is unknown. The one at Mount Vernon is a walnut
period piece (see Illustration 4). Notably missing from the
library inventory is a clock. By 1750 a tall-case clock which
stood on the floor and enclosed the works was the accepted
form. The design followed that of other pieces of furniture with
broken pediments and delicate brass finials. Portable mantel
clocks became available after the Revolution.[26]

4. Copy-press similar to those known to have been used by
George Washington.

Upon retirement Washington wrote:

To Oliver Wolcott
May 15, 1797
To make and sell a little flour, to repair houses going
fast to ruin, to build one for the security of my papers
of a public nature, and to amuse myself with
Agricultural and rural pursuits, will constitute em-
ployment for the years I have to remain on this
terrestrial Globe. If . . I could now and then meet
friends I esteem, it would fill the measure . . . but, if
ever this happens, it must be under my own vine and
fig-tree, as I do not think it probable that I shall go
beyond twenty miles from them.

George Washington spent much of the summer at home in the library preparing his Farewell Address in the manner and arrangement he wished, as it was to be published. In July he executed his last will and testament. He signed his name at the bottom of each of the handwritten pages. The folio pages were left in the desk in the library which suggests the security and privacy of the room while a busy daily usage continued. A thirty-page schedule of crop rotation was made in his own hand during the week before his death. His last letter was to the manager of his estate. He last used the library the day before his death.

Washington is pictured as a model of a country gentleman, virtuous, living in idyllic surroundings.[27] In truth, as exemplified in his library, he was an ordinary man who lived with the commonplace. Building Mount Vernon to his liking was perhaps all the more enjoyable for the little time he had there.

Chapter IV

Washington's Books

					Not in Inventory
Literature	64 items	137 volumes	1 missing		8 additional
Periodicals	36 "	87 "	1 "		5 "
Religious works	35 "	53 "			10 "
Geography and Travels	28 "	62 "			6 "
History	50 "	106 "	17 pamphlets		3 "
Politics, Political Economy, etc.	68 "	88 "	1 pamphlet		3 "
Law	17 "	28 "			4 "
Legislation	26 "	80 "			1 "
Military works	40 "	42 "			6 "
Agriculture	56 "	97 "			1 "
Science	22 "	35 "			1 "
Miscellaneous	21 "	25 "			4 "
Misc. Pamphlets	45 "	53 "			
Maps, charts and prints	53 "				
Total		893 volumes			52 additional

Source: Eugene E. Prussing, **The estate of George Washington, deceased** (Boston: Little, Brown, and Company, 1927), p. 141.

1. Composition of Washington's library by subjects.

The library was Washington's favorite room. It was here that he kept his books, obviously; but also it was a place where he made daily entries in the diaries which he kept most of his life (*"I have a high opinion of beans"* . . . *"of all the amelioriating crops, none in my opinion is equal to potato"*); where he did his accounts; looked over reports from overseers; directed the work of the estate; and wrote his numerous personal and official letters.[1] Here he studied and made notes on republican government which he used when presiding at the Constitutional Convention in 1787,[2] and a study of his correspondence shows that he fairly often quoted from his books in his letters.[3] He made a point of securing the most precise information he could on those topics that interested him; all his life he purchased books.[4] Unfortunately, it is not possible to tell just what books were his favorites (with a few exceptions), partly because after his death the books were widely scattered, but mainly because Washington had no great habit of making marginal notes, underlining, etc., in his books. Overall, though, his library of 800 to 1,000 volumes shows a strong tendency towards practical, even "self-help" books. He also had hundreds of pamphlets, many of them political, and from 200 to 400 folio volumes of his own documents.[5]

Quite commonly books and even whole libraries pass from one generation to the next. In Washington's case only a few books belonging to his father, Augustine Washington, found their way to Mount Vernon. (See Appendix III for inventory of Augustine Washington's library.) Two examples are: *Sermons of the Bishop of Exeter* which has George Washington's youthful signature across the title page,[6] and *Short Discourses upon the Whole Common Prayer*. This latter book has Augustine, Mary, and George Washington's signatures, the latter written when he was thirteen. He also wrote his mother's name below his own and copied his father's signature on the fly leaves.[7]

Biographers, especially in older books on George Washington, have often commented that young George received much of his training from his mother. She is supposed daily to have read from Matthew Hale's *Meditations and Contemplations, Moral and Divine* and then taught him what she had read; from a comparison of copyright dates, this is at least possible. A second book frequently mentioned in this context, James Harvey's *Meditations and Contemplations*, was not published until 1750 when George Washington was eighteen and not living at home. Hale's *Meditations* had originally belonged to Augustine Washington's first wife, Jane Washington, and Mary Ball Washington came across it when she was examining the contents of her new home after she married Augustine. It had the name "Jane Washington" on the flyleaf, and she immediately wrote underneath this "and Mary Washington."[8] This book was one that Washington had at

Mount Vernon and is there now. In addition, the Mount Vernon Ladies' Association owns four other volumes, including *The Female Spectator*, inscribed as having belonged to Mary Ball Washington, but the handwriting is not hers. It is possible that these books actually belonged to her and the signatures were added by other members of the family.

The family Bible, now in the musuem at Mount Vernon, has the inscription:

> George Washington, son to Augustine and Mary his wife, was born the 11th day of February, 1731-2, about ten in the morning, and was baptized the 3rd of April following; Mr. Beverly Whiting and Captain Christopher Brooks, godfathers, and Mrs. Mildred Gregory, godmother.[9] (See Illustration 2).

George Washington's inheritance of books from his parents, then, was fairly meager. Most of his books were gifts or purchases, often ordered from England, in the early years especially:

> The deep Potomac flowed past Mount Vernon, bearing ships of heavy burden to the Chesapeake and overseas; you sent your orders to England every year with your tobacco, and ships returned with the latest modes and manners, books and gazettes, and letters full of coffeehouse gossip.[10]

Unfortunately, we cannot always tell when Washington obtained a particular book, or for that matter when he first used a room at Mount Vernon for a library. The library wing was not finished until 1775, when he was forty-three. A tantalizing early reference of Washington's use of the library has him taking part, on the 9th of July, apparently in 1755, in an engagement at Monongahila, as part of the continuing French and Indian War. He returned home shortly after and wrote a letter to his brother "in his little library there" (at Mount Vernon).[11] As this was twenty years before the addition of the wing which resulted in a library room, we can only conjecture that Washington used, at least before his marriage, one of the four original rooms as a library.

2. George Washington's baptism as recorded in the family Bible.

Lossing remarked in his early monumental work about Mount Vernon that "nearly every work in the collection was of practical value to a man like Washington, and seemed to have been purchased for use as a mechanic would purchase his tools."[12] He found many such books useful, we may assume, in his normal activities at Mount Vernon—books about building, farming, rotation of crops, road building, horticulture, care of cattle, forestry, shrubbery, flowers, horses, and horsemanship.[13] He was known to be well-informed about horses from letters and "deals" he made; and he had *The Compleat Horseman or, Perfect Farrier* by Jacques de Solleysell, published in 1729 (see Illustration 3). In 1759 he obtained Gibson's *Diseases of Horses*. We can only guess how much George Washington's knowledge of horses came from books and how much from experience. Probably it was a mixture of both.

> His orders from booksellers, in the years between Fort Necessity (1754) and the Revolution, show that he read chiefly two classes of books—those about war and those about practical farming.[14]

The earliest evidence of a life-long interest in gardening was in 1759 with an order for Langley's *Book of Gardening*[15] (see Illustration 4). Another volume obtained shortly after his marriage was a small octavo volume, *A New System of Agriculture, or A Speedy Way to Grow Rich*[16] (see Illustration 5). He probably found this much to his taste, although he never grew very rich, his money being invested in Mount Vernon and its farms.

By applying what he read, Washington was instrumental in introducing new methods of agriculture into this country. He was interested not only in farming and gardening, but also in keeping up on the latest developments and discoveries about both. There are numerous references in his diaries and letters to experiments in new methods of agriculture besides his many books on the topic:

THE
Compleat Horseman;
OR,
PERFECT FARRIER.

In TWO PARTS.

PART I. Difcovering the fureft Marks of the Beauty, Goodnefs, Faults, and Imperfections of Horfes; the beft Method of Breeding and Backing of Colts, making their Mouths; Buying, Dieting, and otherwife ordering of Horfes.

The Art of Shoeing, with the feveral forts of Shoes, adapted to the various defects of Bad Feet, and the prefervation of Good.

The Art of Riding and managing the great Horfe, &c.

PART II. Contains the Signs and Caufes of their Difeafes, with the true Method of Curing them.

Written in *French* by the *Sieur de SOLLEYSELL*, Querry to the late King of FRANCE, and one of the Royal Academy of *Paris*.

Abridged from the Folio done into *Englifh* by
Sir *WILLIAM HOPE*.

With the Addition of feveral excellent Receipts, by our beft Farriers: And Directions to the Buyers and Sellers of Horfes.

The FOURTH EDITION Corrected.

Illuftrated with feveral Copper-Plates.

LONDON,
Printed for J. WALTHOE, R. WILKIN, J. and J. BON-WICKE, S. BIRT, T. WARD and E. WICKSTEED, and T. OSBORN. 1729.

3. The kind of practical book Washington liked.

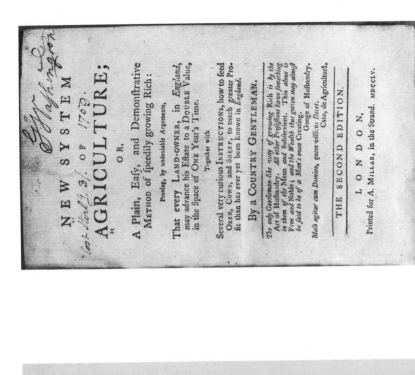

5. A seventeenth-century guide to growing rich.

4. An early example of an interest in gardening books.

If it is not too late in the Season to obtain them I wish you would procure to me in So. Carolina a few of the Acorns of the live Oak and the Seeds of the Evergreen Magnolia; this latter is called in Millers Gardeners dictionary greater Magnolia.

This book now belongs to the Library Company in Philadelphia. When the Mount Vernon kitchen gardens were restored in 1936, books from Washington's library were consulted[17] (see Illustration 6).

In 1760 he tried to order a book whose title he thought was *Hale's Husbandry* but never received anything, so he explained to Robert Cary, his factor in London, that he had just seen a copy of the book and the correct title was *A Compleat Body of Husbandry compiled from the Original Papers of the Late Thomas Hale Esqr.*[18] (see Illustration 7). Present-day librarians may find this a familiar story. A rather rare example of one of Washington's books that has manuscript notes is *Duhamel's Husbandry* published in 1762 by Henri Louis Duhamel Du Monceau (see Illustration 8).

Washington almost certainly purchased a copy of *The Complete Farmer* a few years later, "one of the most popular encyclopedias of husbandry at the time."[19] He was so fond of books of this nature, about agriculture, gardening, husbandry, etc., that they were, according to the inventory made just after his death, kept out on his writing desk.[20]

Washington's concern for his stepchildren, and later his stepgrandchildren, has been the subject of much praise, and he often bought them books. Shortly after he married in 1759, he sent an order to London for *"6 little books for Children begg. to Read,"*[21] for Jacky and Patsy Custis, who were probably six and four respectively at the time. In October, 1761, he wrote to London again and asked for the following to be sent:

M.

MAG

MACALEB. See CERASUS.
MADDER. See RUBIA.
MAGNOLIA. Plum. Nov. Gen. 58. tab. 7.
Plant. 610. The Laurel-leaved Tulip-tree.

The CHARACTERS are,

It is composed of eight or ten oblong, concave, blunt *leaves, hath a great number of short stamina, which are in-* *serted in the germen, and many oblong oval germina, fastened* *together, supporting recurved contorted styles, with hairy* *tops. The germen afterward becomes oval cones, with imbri-* *cated scales, each having one cell, opening with two valves,* *containing a kidney-shaped seed, hanging by a slender thread from* *the top of the cone.*

The SPECIES are,

1. MAGNOLIA (*Glauca*) foliis ovato-lanceolatis subtus glaucis. *Magnolia with oval spear-shaped leaves which are hoary on their under side, and annual; commonly called Small* Magnolia.

2. MAGNOLIA (*Grandiflora*) foliis lanceolatis persisten-tibus caule erecto arboreo. Fig. Plant. tab. 172. *Magnolia with spear-shaped leaves, which are evergreen, and an erect tree; commonly called Great Magnolia.*

3. MAGNOLIA (*Tripetala*) foliis lanceolatis amplissimis basi acutis exterioribus dependentibus. *Magnolia with very large spear-shaped leaves, which are annual, and the flower of the flowers declining; commonly called Umbrella-tree.*

4. MAGNOLIA (*Acuminata*) foliis ovato-lanceolatis acu-minatis, petalis obtusis. *Magnolia with oval, spear-shaped leaves, which are annual, and obtuse petals to the flower.*

The first sort grows pretty common in Virginia and Ca-rolina and other parts of North America. In moist places it rises seven or eight to fifteen or sixteen feet high, the stem is slender. The wood is white and spongy, the bark and of a greenish white colour; the branches are covered with thick smooth leaves, resembling those of the Laurel, but are of an oval shape, smooth on their edges, and hoary underneath. The flowers are produced at the extremity of the branches, which are white, and composed of six or seven petals, and have an agreeable sweet scent. After the fruit increases in size to be as large as a Walnut with its cover, but of a conical shape, having a smooth head round the outside; in each of which is lodged a small seed, about the size of a small Kidney Bean. The seeds are at first green, afterward reds, and when ripe of a scarlet colour. The seeds when ripe, are discharged from the cover, and hang by a slender thread.

These trees are transplanted from the places of their growth, whereby they make handsomer trees, and produce a great number of flowers. This is to be under-stood, for in England they do not thrive so well as in America, as in a moist loamy land.

The second sort grows in Florida and South Carolina, and rises to the height of eighty feet or more, with a straight stem upward of two feet diameter, having a regular

MAG

head. The leaves of this tree resemble those of the com-mon Laurel, but are much larger, and of a lucid green on their upper side, and in some trees are of a russet or buff colour on their under side. These leaves continue all the year, so that this is one of the most beautiful evergreen trees yet known. The flowers are produced at the end of the branches, composed of eight or ten petals, which are narrow at their base, but broad at their extremity, where they are rounded, and a little waved; they are of a purple white colour. In the center is situated a great number of stamina and styles, fastened to one common receptaculum; the flowers are succeeded by oblong scaly cones. These trees, in their native places of growth, begin to produce their flowers in May, which are succeeded by others, so that the woods are perfumed with their odour for a long time; but those which have flowered in England, seldom begin till the middle of June, and do not continue long in beauty. There are many large plants of this sort in the gardens of his Grace the Duke of Richmond, at Goodwood in Sussex, which have produced flowers several years; and in the nursery of the late Mr. Christopher Gray, near Ful-ham, there is one very handsome plant, which has lived in the open air many years, and has abundance of flowers.

As this sort is a native of a warm country, it is a little impatient of cold, especially while young; therefore the plants should be kept in pots, and sheltered in winter for some years, until they have acquired strength, when they may be shaken out of the pots, and planted in the full ground; but they must be planted in a warm situation, where they may be defended from the strong winds, and screened from the north and east, otherwise they will not live abroad.

The third sort grows in Carolina pretty frequent, but in Virginia it is pretty rare. This usually grows from sixteen to twenty feet high, with a slender trunk; the wood is soft and spongy; the leaves of this tree are remarkably large, and are produced in horizontal circles, somewhat resembling an umbrella, from whence the inhabitants of those coun-tries have given it this name. The flowers are composed of ten or eleven white petals, which hang down without any order; the fruit is very like that of the former sort, but longer; the leaves of this sort drop off at the beginning of winter.

This tree is as yet very rare in Europe, but as it is pro-pagated from seeds, we may hope to have it in greater plenty soon, if we can obtain good seeds from Carolina, for it is rarely met with in Virginia.

The fourth sort is also very rare in England. There are but few of the plants at present here, nor is it very common in any of the habitable parts of America; some of these trees have been discovered by Mr. John Bartram, growing on the north branch of Susquehannah river. The leaves of this tree are near eight inches long and five broad, ending in a point. The flowers come out early in the spring, which are composed of twelve white petals, and are shaped

I i i   like

6. Washington quoted from this page of Miller's **Gardener's Dictionary** in a letter.

Agric.

A COMPLEAT BODY

OF

HUSBANDRY.

CONTAINING

RULES for performing, in the moſt profitable
Manner, the whole Buſineſs of the Farmer and
Country Gentleman,

IN

Cultivating, Planting and *Stocking* of Land;

In judging of the ſeveral Kinds of *Seeds,* and of *Manures*; and
in the Management of *Arable* and *Paſture Grounds:*

TOGETHER WITH

The moſt approved Methods of Practice in the ſeveral
Branches of HUSBANDRY,

From ſowing the SEED, to getting in the CROP; and in Breeding
and Preſerving CATTLE, and Curing their DISEASES.

To which is annexed,

The whole Management of the ORCHARD, the
BREWHOUSE, and the DAIRY.

Compiled from the Original Papers of the late
THOMAS HALE, Eſq;

And enlarged by many new and uſeful Communications on
Practical Subjects,

From the Collections of Col. STEVENSON, Mr. RANDOLPH,
Mr. HAWKINS, Mr. STOREY, Mr. OSBORNE, the Reverend
Mr. TURNER, and others.

A WORK founded on Experience; and calculated for general Benefit;
conſiſting chiefly of Improvements made by modern Practitioners in
Farming; and containing many valuable and uſeful Diſcoveries, never
before publiſhed.

ILLUSTRATED WITH

A great Number of CUTS, containing Figures of the Inſtruments of
Huſbandry; of uſeful and poiſonous Plants, and various other Subjects,
engraved from Original Drawings.

Publiſhed by his Majeſty's Royal Licence and Authority.

VOL. I.

THE SECOND EDITION.

LONDON:

Printed for THO. OSBORNE, in Gray's-Inn;
THO. TRYE, near Gray's-Inn Gate Holbourn; and
S. CROWDER and Co. on London-Bridge. MDCCLVIII.

7. Books like Hale's **Husbandry** were kept on the table rather than on the
bookshelves.

A

PRACTICAL TREATISE

O F

HUSBANDRY:

Wherein are contained, many

USEFUL and VALUABLE

EXPERIMENTS and OBSERVATIONS

IN THE

NEW HUSBANDRY,

Collected, during a SERIES of YEARS, by the Celebrated

M. DUHAMEL DU MONCEAU,

Member of the Royal Academy of Sciences at Paris, Fellow of the Royal Society, London, &c,

A L S O,

The moſt approved Practice of the beſt ENGLISH FARMERS, in the OLD METHOD of HUSBANDRY.

W I T H

COPPER-PLATES of ſeveral new and uſeful INSTRUMENTS.

The Second EDITION, corrected and improved.

Agricola incurvo terram dimovit aratio.
Hinc anni labor ; hinc patriam, parvoſque nepotes
Suſtinet ; hinc armenta boum, meritoſque juvencos.

VIRG. Geor. l. 2.

L O N D O N:
Printed for C. HITCH and L. HAWES, J. WHISTON and B. WHITE,
J. RIVINGTON, R. BALDWIN, W. JOHNSTON, S. CROWDER and Co.
and B. LAW and Co.

MDCCLXII

8. Washington jotted notes in the margin of **Duhamel's Husbandry.**

> *A small Bible neatly bound in Turkey, and John Parke*
> *Custis wrote in gilt letters on the inside of the*
> *cover.*
> *A neat, small Prayer Book bound as above, with John*
> *Parke Custis as above.*
> *A neat, small Bible bound in Turkey, and Martha*
> *Parke Custis wrote on the inside in gilt letters.*
> *A small Prayer Book neat and in the same manner.*[22]

On two occasions when Patsy accompanied him and Martha Washington to Williamsburg, they bought her books of songs. (At a much later date he also purchased a French lesson book for his granddaughter, Nelly, who made her home with them.)[23]

At approximately this same time, Washington hired a tutor for Jacky. Soon after his arrival, Washington sent to London for books; these were solely for the study of Latin, the focal point of an upper-class education in the 1700's, which Washington, of course, had not had. The cost of these books was to be divided between Jack and Patsy Custis, both of whom had inherited substantial estates from their father. It is not known whether Patsy was ever actually a pupil with Jack, although the intent seems to have been that she would be. She was afflicted with epilepsy, for which there was no treatment at the time, so this may have prevented it. Later, Greek books were ordered for Jack.[24]

Five years later in 1766, Jack Custis was sent away to school with the Reverend Mr. Jonathan Boucher. Boucher wrote asking that some of Jack's books, including Cicero and Livy, be forwarded. Washington replied that he was sending Cicero's *De Officiis* and also a grammar which Jack had forgotten, but that he could not find the Livy. In July, 1769, he sent to England for over a hundred books to be charged to Jack's account, and therefore presumably for his use. They were chiefly in English and included books on religion, Milton's complete works, Thomson's poems, Hume's and Mrs. Macauley's histories of England, Hooke's *Roman History*, Robertson's *History of Scotland*, Becarria's *Essays on Crimes and Punishments* and several books on composition.[25]

Although not strictly speaking part of the Mount Vernon library, these books are interesting in showing Washington's evident concern over Jack's education, as contrasted with his own rather meager one (see Illustration 9).

A catalogue of the library of Mrs. Washington's first husband, Daniel Parke Custis, was made soon after her marriage to George Washington, who started to initial this inventory with "G.W." for those books he wanted, and "J.C." for those he thought Jack Custis would want.[26] He never finished this, and it is impossible to tell for sure how many of the books were ever at Mount Vernon, but they perhaps made up another source of books for Washington's library (see Appendix IV). One such book, *The Second Volume of the Posthumous Works of Mr. Samuel Butler*, has the signature of Jn⁰ Custis on the title page and "George Washington Parke Custis at Vernon Mount," on the fly leaf. Jonathan Custis was Daniel Parke Custis' father, and George Washington Parke Custis was Martha Washington's grandson, which evidently means that at least one Custis book found its way to Mount Vernon. A copy of *The Family Physician and the House Apothecary* with the autograph of John Custis on the title page is sometimes listed as a probable book belonging to George Washington.

George Washington seems not to have read novels a lot, which may have been partly because there were not many novels written at that time, and also because his interests were more pragmatic. There is only one American novel in the known books of his library, *The Foresters* by Jeremy Belknap; but he did have quite a bit of American poetry and also some English and European fiction familiar to today's readers, such as *Don Quixote*, some Shakespeare, *Tom Jones*, *Robinson Crusoe*, and *Gulliver's Travels*, which he may have had as a child.[27]

In 1751 at the age of twenty, he bought a copy of *The Adventures of Peregrine Pickle* by Tobias Smollett, a satire of English life and social customs.[28] Originally consisting of three volumes, the work also contains "Memoirs of a Lady of Quality," with Washington's autographs on the title pages (see Illustration 10).

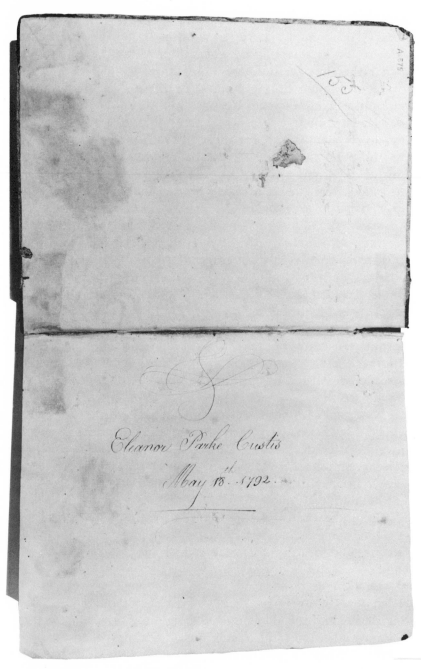

9. Child's book used at Mount Vernon

THE ADVENTURES

OF

Peregrine Pickle.

In which are included,

MEMOIRS

OF A

LADY OF QUALITY.

By the AUTHOR of

RODERICK RANDOM.

VOL. II.

Respicere exemplar vitæ morumque jubebo
Doctum imitatorem, & veras hinc ducere voces.
                                                    HOR.

DUBLIN:

Printed for ROBERT MAIN, Bookfeller in
Dame-Street, oppofite to *Fownes's-Street*.
MDCCLI.

10. Early purchase of a novel.

During the 1760's a number of people important to the development of the emerging nation visited Mount Vernon, and Washington also carried on a voluminous correspondence with a great many people all his life.[29] The effects and influences of these visits and letters are outside the scope of this work, but we may certainly picture both the talks with distinguished visitors and the letter-writing as taking place in whatever room Washington was using as a library or study at the time; his growing collection of books, plus the work inherent in managing his estate, indicate that some room must have been used for this purpose during the period 1755-1775.

In 1763 *A New and Complete Dictionary of Arts and Sciences, Comprehending all the Branches of Useful Knowledge* was published in London (see Illustration 11). This four-volume set, actually a sort of encyclopedia of art and science in the 1700's, was one of only a relatively few reference books that Washington owned. It consisted of excerpts from "the best authors in all languages." Each volume has Washington's book-plate and autograph.

Washington had become friendly with George Mason, who lived in nearby Gunston Hall. Mason was a scholar and a reader, with a good library, who may have encouraged Washington in his reading, at least by example. The two continued to visit back and forth for many years, and we can probably accurately picture them as meeting in the library of one or the other to talk about the evolving of the new nation. Also, Mason's cousin, James Mercer, had a library at his plantation; he and Mason loaned books back and forth, so Washington may have seen and used books at either place. In 1774 Washington and Mason were among the leaders of the opposition of the American colonies against England. They had conferences together at both Mount Vernon and Gunston Hall, most likely in the library at the latter, and the result was the Virginia Resolves, attributed to Mason, which may have been the inspiration for the Declaration of Independence.[30] On August 31, 1774, according to Lossing, Patrick Henry and Edmund Pendleton came to Mount Vernon and spent the whole day in the library, leaving the next day for the Continental Congress in Philadelphia.[31] Since the library wing was not

11. Volume I of the four-volume encyclopedia of art and science in the seventeenth century.

completed until the next year, some other room must have been used for this purpose. Lossing also refers to Washington's rising early and spending several hours in the library "in the year before the War,"[32] which would also indicate another room was used.

When he assumed command of the Revolutionary Army in June of 1775, Washington, of course, was away from Mount Vernon almost continuously for eight years. During this period he read military manuals from abroad (and also asked questions of people he considered well-informed)[33] to help him in commanding the army (see Illustration 12). In his Orderly Book of May 8, 1777, we find him recommending that his officers should make use of their leisure time to study military authors, so presumably he had found his own study helpful:

> *Officers attentive to their duty, will find abundant employment in training and disciplining their men, providing for them, and seeking that they appear neat, clean and soldier-like. Nor will anything redound more to their honor—afford them more solid amusement, or better answer the end of their appointment, than to devote the vacant moments, they may have to the study of military authors.*

In the early days of the War, the British planned to lay waste the towns and country along the Potomac, including Mount Vernon, which was to be burned. General Dunmore's plans were defeated by an American militia company and a bad storm. Mrs. Washington packed her husband's papers, the silver, and other valuables, and left for one night.[34] No attempt seems to have been made to save any of the books, which is interesting in view of the fact that there are numerous accounts of public and private libraries being deliberately destroyed by an army in wartime. Again, in 1781, Alexandria and Mount Vernon were alarmed by the appearance of British men-of-war. Washington's manager, Lund Washington, went on board and offered provisions, with the result that some other houses were burnt but Mount Vernon was spared.[35] Washington indicated his anger at this in a letter to Lund.

REGULATIONS

FOR THE

Order and Difcipline

OF THE

TROOPS

OF THE

UNITED STATES.

by
Ǥ. W. A. H. Ǥ., Baron Steuben

PART I.

PHILADELPHIA:

Printed by STYNER and CIST, in Second-ftreet.
M DCC LXXIX.

12. Washington read books like this to help him in the command of the Revolutionary Army.

In his somewhat tongue-in-cheek book, Kitman says that one of the most frequently read books in Washington's library was *Book-Keeping Moderniz'd: Or, Merchants Accounts by Double Entry, according to the Italian Form*[36] (see Illustration 13). Without discussing his contention that Washington used his Revolutionary War expense account to his own advantage, it must be pointed out that it is difficult to see how the sixth edition of *Book-Keeping Moderniz'd*, dated 1793, could have been of much help during the Revolutionary War from 1775-1783. This book, with Washington's autograph, is now in the Boston Athenaeum. It is not an unreasonable assumption that something of this nature would have been helpful in the running of Mount Vernon with its five farms and extensive staff. It certainly is the type of practical book that Washington often liked.

Evidently Washington was at Mount Vernon at least briefly during the War, in 1781, since he entertained De Chastellaux, a French nobleman who accompanied Rochambeau to America to help in the struggle of the colonies against Great Britain. Their meeting took place in the library, and from there Washington wrote a bantering letter to De Chastellaux six years later congratulating him on his marriage.[31] De Chastellaux later wrote a book about his travels in North America, which Washington had in both French and English (see Illustration 14).

Earlier, in 1759, the Reverend Andrew Burnaby, archdeacon of Leicester, had visited Washington at Mount Vernon; he included a brief description of the view from the house in his *Travels Through the Middle Settlements of North America in 1754-1760*, which was published in 1775. "For its time, Washington's library at Mount Vernon was exceedingly well stocked with historical works as well as books relating to geography and travel."[38] Mrs. Washington apparently shared this interest, since a copy of *Embassy to China*, a book about the land and people of China as well as about the embassy, was purchased for her in 1796. Washington was also fond of the theatre and owned some copies of plays.

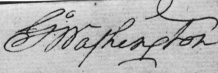

BOOK-KEEPING MODERNIZ'D:

O R,

MERCHANT-ACCOUNTS by DOUBLE ENTRY, according to the ITALIAN Form.

WHEREIN

The THEORY of the ART is clearly explained, and reduced to PRACTICE, in copious SETS OF BOOKS, exhibiting all the Varieties that ufually occur in Real Bufinefs.

To which is added,

A Large APPENDIX.

CONTAINING,

I. Defcriptions and fpecimens of the Subfidiary Books ufed by Merchants.
II. Monies and Exchanges, the nature of Bills of Exchange, Promiffory Notes, and Bills of Parcels.
III. Precedents of Merchants Writings, peculiar to England, Scotland, and common to both.
IV. The Commiffion, Duty, and Power of Factors.
V. A fhort Hiftory of the Trading Companies in Great Britain, with an account of her exports and imports.
VI. The produce and commerce of the Sugar Colonies; with a fpecimen of

the accounts kept by the factors or ftorekeepers; and an explication of wharf and plantation accounts.
VII. The produce and commerce of the Tobacco Colonies; with a fpecimen of the accounts ufually kept by the ftorekeepers.
VIII. The method of keeping accounts proper for Shop-keepers or Retailers.
IX. The method of keeping the accounts of a Land eftate.
X. A Dictionary, explaining abftrufe words and terms that occur in merchandife.

By JOHN MAIR, A.M.

The SIXTH EDITION.

EDINBURGH:

Printed for BELL & BRADFUTE, and WILLIAM CREECH; And fold by T. LONGMAN, G. G. J. & J. ROBINSON, T. CADELL, and C. DILLY, London.

MDCCXCIII.

13. A useful guide to double-entry accounting; Washington liked practical books like this.

G:Washington

TRAVELS

I N

NORTH-AMERICA,

IN THE YEARS 1780, 1781, AND 1782.

BY THE

MARQUIS DE CHASTELLUX,

ONE OF THE FORTY MEMBERS OF THE FRENCH
ACADEMY, AND MAJOR GENERAL IN THE
FRENCH ARMY, SERVING UNDER THE COUNT
DE ROCHAMBEAU.

TRANSLATED FROM THE FRENCH
BY AN ENGLISH GENTLEMAN,
WHO RESIDED IN AMERICA AT THAT PERIOD.

WITH NOTES BY THE TRANSLATOR.

Πολλων δ'ανθρωπων ιδεν αστεα και νοον εγνω. Odyſſey. B. I.

Multorumque hominum vidit urbes, & mores cognovit.

VOLUME II.

LONDON:
PRINTED FOR G. G. J. AND J. ROBINSON,
PATER-NOSTER ROW.
M DCC LXXXVII.

14. Both George and Martha Washington enjoyed travel books.

On September 18th, 1782, the inventory of the library then remaining of John Parke Custis, Mrs. Washington's late son, was filed in Fairfax County by Lund Washington. It contained 327 titles [39] (see Appendix V). It is not known whether these books were part of the Mount Vernon library. On July 23, 1783, Lund made an inventory of the Mount Vernon library which he sent on to Washington in Newburgh. Incomprehensively, this list has only sixty entries plus "several" titles that Lund did not think worth listing. Washington added his note at the end that it was an accurate list and instructed Lund to see if any of his books were at Abingdon, a Custis home on the Potomac about fifteen miles north of Mount Vernon. If Washington really had only about sixty books in 1783, when he was fifty-one and his library wing had been finished for eight years, he must have greatly increased his holdings in the years between the end of the War and his death in 1799. Many of the books he was known to have obtained before 1783 are in fact on the list (see Appendix VI).

One further category might be added to Washington's acquisition of books: those which belonged to Martha Washington either before or after their marriage in 1759. In the fall of 1758 Martha Dandridge Custis sent an order to her factor in London. (This was the same Robert Cary who was Washington's factor.) In the order she asked for *A Song Book . . .Choice Collection of New Songs*. This entry was crossed out, however, and further down the title *The Bull-Finch* is found, possibly indicating that the correct title was ascertained before the order went out. Besides the *Bull-Finch*, Cary was to get two other song books and *Muses Delight* by Sadler. The order for *Bull-Finch*, a collection of 400 love songs of various types, was filled, but *Muses Delight* was not available; the former was well-known in both England and Virginia and it had been sold in Williamsburg in February of the same year. It first appeared about 1748 and went through a dozen editions and had various publishers. This is probably the 1757 edition (see Illustration 15). The order was received on March 1, 1759, after the marriage of George Washington and Martha Dandridge Custis on January 6th of that year. On the title page is inscribed "Martha Washington" and the date, 1759, both written by George Washington. A copy of *Tea Table Miscellany* has the

15. Frontispiece from one of Mrs. Washington's books.

signature "Martha Parke Custis" and the date 1768.[40]

One similar interesting example is *The Letters of the Late Rev. Laurence Sterne, to his most Intimate Friends. With fragments in the manner of Rabelais . . . Three volumes bound in one*, Dublin, 1776. On the flyleaf of this book is the autograph "M. Washington" and on the first page of the dedication is "Washington" in her handwriting. It is referred to as her book, but we can only conjecture which of them purchased it and read it, possibly both. Martha Washington did enjoy and read *Children of the Abbey* by Regina Maria Roche. Recently the Mount Vernon Ladies' Association acquired the letter in which Martha Washington ordered it, and Volumes 3 and 4 of it are now in the mansion library with a note by her granddaughter, Eleanor Parke Custis, that her grandmother read and liked it. There are also extant several almanacs with diary annotations by Martha Washington, a leather-bound memorandum with her notes in it, two prayer books, a Bible, and a cookbook by Hannah Glass, all of which belonged to her.

In anticipation of returning to Mount Vernon on Christmas Eve, 1783, Washington bought a selection of toys and children's books for his stepgrandchildren.[41] Mrs. Washington's son, John Parke Custis, had died in 1781, and she and General Washington had adopted two of his children. The tutor for the grandchildren was Gideon Snow, who was probably the first to use the little octagon house in the Mount Vernon garden as a schoolhouse.[42] It is not known whether Washington ordered school or other books for these children. Those books left from Jack and Patsy's childhood may have served. Around 1784 he ordered a quantity of books, including travel narratives, for the leisure he expected to have.[43]

There followed a period of living at his beloved Mount Vernon again, from 1783 to 1789, where Washington rose before dawn and wrote letters or read in his library until breakfast. After a daily tour of his grounds, he returned to the library until dinner at 3 o'clock.[44] He was busy ordering books as his correspondence shows (see Illustration 16). In the late 1770's Mawe's *Universal Gardener and Botanist* was published, so Washington was able to secure another of the sort of book he

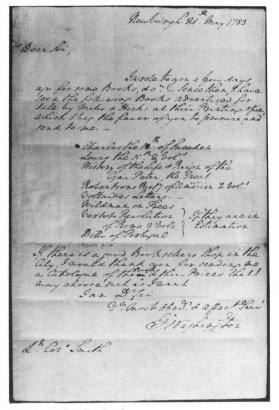

16. An order for books.

liked so much (see Illustration 17). This general dictionary of gardening and botany probably became one of his favorite books. In 1785 a visitor to Mount Vernon said that Washington's greatest pride was to be thought the first farmer in America.[45]

Then in 1787 Washington went to Philadelphia as a delegate to the Constitutional Convention. He immediately began a study of constitutional government, including two subscriptions to *The Federalist*, in which Madison, Jay, and Hamilton defended the Constitution. He had one set bound for his library at Mount Vernon and sent the others on, presumably to people he thought would be interested. He carried on a copious correspondence all his life, as has been noted, and during the 1780's these letters were often concerned with the idea of the Constitution.[46]

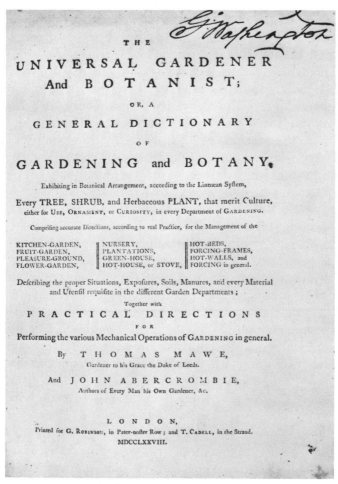

17. Title page from **Universal Gardener**, a dictionary of gardening and botany.

In 1786 *Lyric Works of Horace, by a Native American* by John Parke was published in Philadelphia. Parke was a Revolutionary officer and poet who dedicated two books to Washington. Besides the translation of Homer, the book contained several poems, including "Virginia," which was a pastoral drama composed for George Washington's birthday and set at Mount Vernon. The author sent a copy to Washington, who wrote a letter of acknowledgement saying, "*I always wish to give every possible encouragement to those works of genius which are the production of an American.*"

This is an indication of the growth of American publishing and the gradual shift from the earlier dependence of Virginia on imported books from England.

The United States Senate was organized on the 6th of April, 1789. As soon as the votes of the electoral college could be opened and counted, official notification was sent to Washington by Charles Thomson, who arrived at Mount Vernon on the morning of April 14th. Washington took him to the library where the news that he was to be the first president was imparted. After dinner, Washington went to "his private study in an upper room" where he wrote an acceptance letter.[47] Again, we can only conjecture as to which room this was.

Washington went to New York to start his first term as president, and, following his lifelong habit of reading for specific purposes, he read extensively from the papers of the confederation period and used them for guidance in establishing a precedent for succeeding presidents with no real guidelines to follow.[48] He had quite a few books on politics, and also a considerable number of pamphlets on the same subject, but few philosophical works except those on politics.[49] During his two terms as president, he visited Mount Vernon for varying periods of time, occasionally for as long as two months, often for a few days. While there, he kept up with his letters and other paper work by working in the library for several hours every day.[50]

Franklin's Library Company was housed in Carpenter's Hall in Philadelphia, which had become the national capitol. Members of Congress were allowed to borrow books, a courtesy for which Washington sent a letter of thanks in 1791. After his second term as president had ended, he was given, in 1797, library privileges and a specially bound catalogue of the collection.[51] His copy of the *Philadelphia Directory* of 1796 shows Washington's address as 190 High Street (see Illustration 18). Washington was a Mason, and in 1793 he received five volumes of *Sentimental and Masonic Magazine* from its proprietor.[52]

In the summer of 1796, anticipating his retirement from the presidency at the end of his second term, Washington was at Mount Vernon and worked in the library on the final draft of

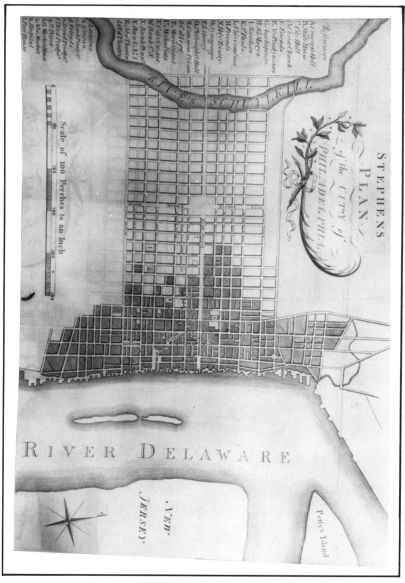

18. Washington lived at 190 High Street in Philadelphia when he was president, as shown in the **Philadelphia Directory.**

his famous Farewell Address, to which Hamilton, Jay, and Madison had contributed in both oral and written form.[53] Following the end of his presidency, he returned to Mount Vernon in 1797 and took up the strands of the life he really loved. Before leaving Philadelphia, he purchased *The Vicar of Wakefield* (a fairly unusual example of his buying a novel) and Buffon's *Natural History*,[54] but he wrote on May 29, 1797, to James McHenry:

> *But it may strike you that in this detail no mention is made of any portion of time allotted for reading. The remark would be just, for I have not looked into a book since I came home; nor shall I be able to do it until I have discharged my workmen;* (He was having repairs made to Mount Vernon.)

The sentence goes on to conclude rather gloomily that he may have more time to read when the nights grow longer, but by then, *"I may be looking in Doomsday Book."* As a matter of fact, he did find some time for reading again (see Illustration 19).

On July 17, 1797, Washington wrote a letter to Col. Timothy Pickering from Mount Vernon:

> *The Journals of the 1st, 2nd & 3rd Sessions of the first Congress, I have, & no later—These are in folio—one volume of the Senate, and another of the House of Representatives—If no complete set can be had, either in folio or octavo, It would be useless to obtain a copy of what I now possess; but if they are to be continued in the latter, and an entire set could be had of that size it would be preferred on account of uniformity.— Please to accompany the copying press with the account of cost, & the amount shall be transmitted in bank notes.*

Evidently Washington was concerned with acquiring books in matching sets, a fairly common practice of the time. People often had books bound to order to match other books in their libraries from the 1630's to the 1830's. Leather (morocco, calf, sheep) was used,[55] and the tooling was elaborate (see Illustration 20). Washington owned leather-bound volumes of Gib-

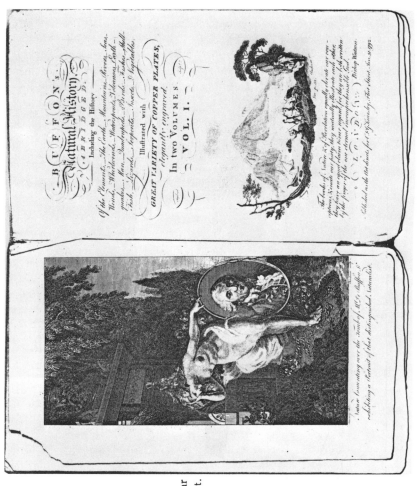

19. Washington bought **Natural History** near the end of his second term as president.

20. One of Washington's calf-bound books with gilt ornamentation.

bon's *Decline and Fall of the Roman Empire* with hand tooling, and his copy of *The Poems of Ossian, Son of Fingal* was probably bound especially for him in calf, with an American eagle and other designs in gilt on the back.

Washington was the recipient of a good many books in his life, especially in his later years, both in sets and in single volumes. These were not of his selection. Especially after he became prominent, a good many authors sent him their own books which they asked him to sponsor although sometimes the books were sent by other than their authors. On May 9, 1794, Washington sent a letter to the Rev. Mr. Jeremy Belknap from Philadelphia, where he was visiting:

> *Your letter of the 14th unto. and the first vol. of an American Biography, came safe to my hands. For both I pray you to accept my thanks, — and to consider me as a subscriber to the latter.*

The *American Biography* eventually consisted of four volumes, all of which Washington had.

On July 9, 1795, he wrote from Philadelphia to James Renwell, Esq.:

> *I have been favored with your letter of the 29th of April accompanying your memoir of a Map of Hindoostan, with engravings, etc.—for your kindness in sending which I entreat you to accept my best thanks.*

Whether or not Washington had any interest in a map of India, or whether he had perhaps requested either it or the *American Biography*, cannot now be determined. He may very possibly have had an interest in a biography of famous Americans, many of whom were his friends, and his early surveying experiences, during which he often made maps, might have made the *Map of Hindoostan* of some interest. Both letters read rather more as polite thank-you notes for unsolicited gifts. Good manners may well have compelled him to respond civilly to any such gifts. The very next day, July 10, 1795, he wrote to the Revd. Mr. C. Cruttwell to thank him for a copy of the works of the Bishop of London & Man, which had been sent to him in the will of Dr. Thomas Wilson.[56] The tone of the letter suggests that this was a polite reply to a bequest that he could hardly have gracefully refused. He was probably more genuinely pleased by a gift from Sir John Sinclair which he acknowledged in a letter written from Mount Vernon on July 15, 1797, thanking him for

> *your printed account of the origin of the Board of Agriculture and its progress. . . I will keep one copy of this work myself, and shall read it, I am sure with pleasure, so soon as I have passed through my harvest, which is now nearly finished—the other copies shall be put into such hands as I conceive will turn them to the best account.*

It would be interesting to know just how many copies Sir John had sent; it is typical of Washington to finish the harvest before getting on with his reading, but the topic is one likely to interest him. He also seems to have received a copy of Euripides from Lord Cornwallis about this time. He had defeated Cornwallis at Yorktown, which ended the Revolutionary War, and the two were not friends, so this gift is something of a puzzle.

To return to Washington's interest in gardening, when the famous architect Latrobe came to visit Mount Vernon in 1796, he disliked the parterres (ornamental arrangements of flower beds in different sizes and shapes) in front of the greenhouse, which were trimmed into fleur-de-lis. Latrobe thought these pedantic, and they may in fact have been copied from one of Washington's horticulture books by a gardener.[57] On the other hand, Washington was a great admirer of France and Frenchmen, like his good friend LaFayette, so this influence may have been the source of the fleur-de-lis.

On August 31, 1797, Washington wrote to David Longworth to thank him for the first volume of *Telemachus* that Longworth had published and to subscribe for the second volume. From the frequency that this was done, it is tempting to think that people had found that if you sent Washington the first volume of something, he would subscribe to the subsequent volume(s). As an interesting sidelight to the growth of printing in this country, Longworth reported that he tried a new method of "hot pressing" in the printing of *Telemachus*, which, he took pains to point out in a letter to Washington, was entirely American.

One of the last books that Washington obtained was *Essays and Notes on Husbandry* by J. B. Bordley, copyrighted in 1799, the year of Washington's death (see Illustration 21). Reflecting again Washington's interest in farming, his *"occupational preference and abiding interest,"* the book is inscribed "To his Excellency General George Washington from his obedient and humble servant, the Author." Bordley was a lawyer and farmer himself, and the two were friends. Bordley had previously published some agricultural pamphlets and always sent his publications to Washington, who almost certainly enjoyed them. They also corresponded about farming and exchanged samples of grain, for Bordley was as interested as Washington in experimental agriculture. Here was a book after Washington's own heart.

> In what he called his Botanical Garden, between the flower-garden and the spinner's house, Washington carried on much of his investigation. The nurseries, gardens, and greenhouse were filled with choice collections of rare plants, fruit trees, vegetables and flowers. To do this was not easy at a time when means of communication and transportation were almost primitive, but admirers in all parts of the world knew that the best way to please the most distinguished man in the world was to send him a choice plant or animal for his estate. Washington's favorite Bible quotation about the shade of his own vine and fig-tree was not entirely a figure of speech, for fig-trees were trained on the warm side of the north garden wall, and he paid much attention to the cultivation of grapes. It is not in accordance with his character that the story by which Washington is most widely known represents him as wantonly destroying a cherry tree. In later years he wrote: *"It is always in one's power to cut a tree down, but time only can place them where one would have them."* The passages in Washington's letters and diaries, in which he spoke of his trees,

G Washington

ESSAYS AND NOTES

O N

HUSBANDRY

AND

RURAL AFFAIRS.

By J. B. BORDLEY.

Still let me COUNTRY CULTURE fcan :
My FARM's my Home : " My Brother, MAN :
" And GOD is every where."

PHILADELPHIA :

PRINTED BY BUDD AND BARTRAM,

FOR THOMAS DOBSON, AT THE STONE HOUSE,
No 41, SOUTH SECOND STREET.

1799.
[*Copy-Right Secured according to Law.*]

21. Title page of a volume on General Washington's favorite subject with his customary signature denoting ownership.

would make a book of considerable size. The last time he left the house, which was the afternoon of the day before he died, he walked out through the snow to mark some trees to be cut down between mansion and river. One of his last letters was to his manager about the care of Mount Vernon. At his death he left written plans for the rotation of crops up the end of 1803.[58]

Washington's stepgranddaughter (and adopted daughter), Eleanor Parke (Nelly) Custis was married to his nephew Lawrence Lewis at Mount Vernon in 1799 on Washington's birthday, and he gave the minister who performed the ceremony a copy of Catherine Macauley's *History of England* in eight volumes, with the following interesting inscription:

These, sir, were written by a remarkable lady, who visited America many years ago; and here is also her treatise on the Immutability of Moral Truth, which she sent me just before her death—read it and return it to me.

This is a most unusual instance of Washington's loaning a book, a practice common enough at the time, but one in which he seems to have indulged very little. A few months later, he gave two volumes of his six-volume set of *The Botanical Magazine, or Garden Displayed* by William Custis to Nelly (see Color Plate XIII). She and her husband were to receive the land for the plantation they built, Woodlawn, and these illustrated books told how to choose and cultivate flowers and shrubs.[59]

On July 3rd, 1799, Washington wrote the following printed announcement, which is pasted inside the front cover of his copy of *The Immortal Mentor*, edited by Mason Weems, later the author of the famous biography of Washington which included a number of made-up stories such as the cherry-tree story.

RECOMMENDATION
By GEORGE WASHINGTON
Mount Vernon, July 3rd, 1799

Rev. Sir,

For your kind compliment—"The Immortal Mentor,"
I beg you to accept my best thanks. I have perused it
with singular satisfaction; and hesitate not to say that
it is, in my opinion at least, an invaluable com-
pilation. I cannot but hope that a book whose con-
tents do such credit to its title, will meet a very
generous patronage.

Should that patronage equal my wishes, you will have
no reason to regret that you ever printed the Immortal
Mentor.

With respect I am Rev. Sir,
Your most obedient
Humble Servant,
GEORGE WASHINGTON

When he died in 1799, George Washington had from 800 to 1,000 books, rather more than the "handful of treatises" sometimes credited him[60] (see Appendix II). The difference in count is determined by which inventory one uses. Also, Washington's unpublished correspondence shows books not on any inventory.[61] It is not known how this many books were accommodated on shelves built for about 300 books; Washington may have used the cupboards by the fireplace, the floor, the closet, or double-shelving.

Washington's will was a lengthy one with a number of detailed bequests. In the matter of Mount Vernon and its contents, however, he simply left it all to his wife, Martha Washington, with his nephew Bushrod Washington, the son of his brother Jack and a justice of the Supreme Court, the heir after her death. Bushrod inherited Mount Vernon in 1802 only three years later when Mrs. Washington died; he also received all of George Washington's papers, civil, military, and private, and *"at the decease of my wife and before if she is not inclined to retain them I give and bequeath [to Bushrod] my library of books and pamphlets of every kind."*

An extensive inventory was made of the contents in each room of the house. This appraiser's inventory listed 884 volumes, not counting pamphlets, but was not an accurate record of all the books Washington ever owned. With Mrs. Washington's consent Bushrod could have taken possession of the books and papers before 1802, but he apparently made no request to do so. Mrs. Washington's will made provision for the rest of the contents of the house to be given or sold to relatives, but the books stayed there when Bushrod took possession. She left her personal books of every kind except a large Bible and a prayer book to her grandson, G. W. P. Custis.

Actually Washington may have had no real right to leave Mount Vernon to anyone, as his brother Lawrence's will had stipulated that if George died without issue, as he did, the original 2,500 acres of Mount Vernon were then to go to Augustine Washington (Lawrence's full brother) or his heirs. Such entails were legal during part of George Washington's life, but the law was changed before he died, so the question of whether Mount Vernon was his to dispose of or not is uncertain. In any event, Augustine's heirs never contested the will, possibly because there was a law that a person could not both benefit under and contest the same will, and they had inherited other land from Washington's will,[62] or possibly because they preferred to honor their uncle's wishes (and avoid a family quarrel).

At any rate Bushrod came to live at Mount Vernon, and a correspondent in 1822 said George Washington's library contained a large and handsome collection of books. The papers were rather casually disposed of by Bushrod who gave them away to autograph seekers, loaned them indefinitely to people writing about his uncle, and allowed copies to be made and the originals removed.

When Bushrod died in 1829, he had nearly doubled the size of the collection of books. His nephew, George Corbin Washington, inherited Mount Vernon, what was left of the papers, and all the books in the library *except* the law books (which were probably Bushrod's additions to the library). The law books went to Bushrod's grandnephew, Bushrod Washington Herbert, who was studying law, and 468 volumes in the dining room went to another nephew, John Augustine Washington.[63] In 1834 the United States government bought the manuscripts and papers and most of the military books for $25,000.[64] In 1848 either Senator Pearce or Jared Sparks, author of *The Writings of Washington*, suggested to George Corbin Washington that he might be interested in selling his portion of Washington's books to the Library of Congress, but he had just sold most of them for $3,000 to a bookseller, Henry Stevens, who had a commission to buy a copy of every American book the British Museum did not already possess.[65] The books which Stevens acquired consisted of 460 volumes, 359 of which were George Washington's, and about 750 pamphlets, of which 450 belonged to George Washington.

Stevens took the collection to New York for storage, where he offered 300 of the books with Washington's autograph to a well-known book collector named James Lenox, who did not purchase any of them. He then offered them to the British Museum, but national sentiment had been aroused over sending them out of the country. Stevens offered them to a group of Bostonians for $7,500 if the British Museum did not take them. (The Senate also directed the Committee on the Library of Congress to look into purchasing them but nothing ever came of it.) Stevens lowered his price to $5,000 since the money had to be raised by subscriptions of fifty dollars each. Only $3,250 was raised, and Stevens needed ready cash, so he rather bitterly agreed to let the books go for that. He retained five books with the best autographs, two of which he sold to Lenox; he presented the remaining three to the British Museum, the Bodleian, and the Royal Library of Berlin, leaving 354. Since the Boston Athenaeum had subscribed $500 to the fund and since most of the subscribers were Proprietors of the Boston Athenaeum, the books were housed there permanently although Stevens had expected them to go to Harvard.[66] There are also twenty-one volumes in the Harkness Collection of the New York Public Library and eight in the Huntington Library. The collection in the Athenaeum remains intact; it is divided into four parts: I. Books from the library of General George Washington. II. Other books from Mount Vernon. III. The Writings of Washington. IV. Washingtoniana.

It is not known what happened to the rest of the books left to George Corbin Washington. The books that had been left to John A. Washington passed to his heirs, and a small collection was sold some years after the Stevens' sale. Later, in 1876, 282 volumes were sent to the Philadelphia Centennial Exposition and then sold.[67] Most of these were purchased by John R. Baker of Philadelphia whose library in turn was sold in 1901. Also in the 1890's there were at least five sales of Washington's books, from various branches of the family.[68] Probably those law books inherited by Bushrod Washington Herbert included few if any of George Washington's books, but it is not known what happened to these books. The inventory of the library of Eleanor Parke Custis and Lawrence Lewis at Woodlawn probably includes a number of George Washington's books.[69]

The Mount Vernon Ladies' Association began restoring the library at Mount Vernon in 1929 after it was assigned to the Vice Regent from Massachusetts in 1880; virtually all the books were gone by this time. The first books were restored shortly thereafter, and each year sees some new acquisitions. In 1936 there were twenty-nine original volumes at Mount Vernon, and the annual reports of the Mount Vernon Ladies' Association show new original books acquired nearly every year. There are now seventy-five to eighty originals at Mount Vernon and between 400 and 600 duplicates. Because so many of the books are permanently in the Anthenaeum, in 1950 the decision was made to substitute duplicate editions whenever possible. Actual Washington books still occasionally surface. Their price is now quite high, from $2,000-$5,000 for originals. Duplicates generally cost from $20-$125.

Some, although by no means all, of Washington's books contain his bookplate which he ordered through Robert Adams on November 22, 1771 (see Illustration 22).

It was engraved in London by S. Valliscure at the cost of fourteen shillings, with an additional cost of six shillings for making 300 impressions. These were shipped on March 25, 1772, and reached Washington later that year. The bookplate has the armorial bearings of the Washington family and the motto: *"Exitus Acto Probat"* — *"the end justifies the means,"* or *"the end shows the deed,"* or *"the result proves [or tests] the*

EXITUS ACTA PROBAT

George Washington

22. Even the inexperienced eye can detect the difference between the real and spurious bookplate. This is the genuine one.

act," and the name *"George Washington"* in script.[70] This motto has not definitely been established as belonging to the Washington family. He added to the ornamentation around the coat of arms some spears of wheat to indicate *"the most favorite amusement of my life."*[71] It was counterfeited at least once and about 200 volumes with the false bookplate were offered for sale in 1863, but the forgery was detected before the sale (see Illustration 23). Books with spurious bookplates are still tur-

EXITUS ACTA PROBAT

George Washington

23. The counterfeit bookplate.

ning up. Of the 884 volumes in the Appraisers Inventory, 137 have the genuine bookplate. Washington also often wrote his name in the upper right corner of the title page or sometimes on the first page of the preface or of the text.[72]

There is really no indication of just what purpose, if any, Washington had in mind for his books to serve after his death. Notable collections of books have been given to some public use after the death of their owners since John Harvard made his bequest. Most of the large libraries of 1500-1700 were collected to save good books for the future.[73] Public and college libraries all over the country owe their inception, at least, to the philanthropy of some donor, and the practice continues, particularly in the area of "special collections."[74] Washington made no attempt to do this; the most we can say is that Bushrod as a Supreme Court justice may have found the books useful, but even this is tenuous, and we have no clue as to what was in Washington's mind. He seems not to have collected books for their use to future generations, just as he seems not to have loaned (or borrowed) books in the manner that was so common among his contemporaries.

There is little doubt that Washington was genuinely interested in encouraging education. He sent a number of his young relatives to school at his expense besides his stepchildren and stepgrandchildren. He even sent a few friends' children to school, even though they were no relation of his. On June 15, 1774, he dined at a Mrs. Dawson's and spent the evening at the capitol at a meeting of the Society for Promoting Useful Knowledge. He had in the preceding year subscribed ten shillings to the society, and on the occasion mentioned above he gave it L1.[75] On August 18, 1782, he sent a letter to President William Smith of Washington College in Chestertown thanking Smith for naming the college after him and offering a gift of fifty guineas.

> When that period shall arrive, when we can hail the blest return of peace, it will add to my pleasure to see this infant seat of learning rising into consistency and proficiency in the sciences, under the nurturing hands of its founders.

Washington, John Adams, and Aaron Burr are thought to have contributed to the infant "Transylvania Library," chartered in 1795, which was the beginning of the Lexington Public Library.[76]

In his annual addresses to Congress while president, he urged the support of education and science and suggested the establishment of a national university. He observed that the existing institutions lacked the money necessary to obtain *"the ablest professors in the different departments of liberal knowledge."* In his later years particularly, he espoused the cause of creating a national university in Washington, D.C.. From 1794 on, he corresponded about this to John Adams, Edmond Randolph, Alexander Hamilton, and Thomas Jefferson, and in 1795 he proposed it to the Commissioners of the District of Columbia, as well as advising it in his messages to Congress.[77] (Earlier, in 1788, he had shown an interest in a proposal for a universal language in the hope that if it were successful this would *"one day remove many of the causes of hostility from amongst mankind."*) He suggested to Hamilton that such a university would be a place where students from all over the country could *"receive the polish of Erudition in the Arts, Sciences and Belles Lettres."* He hoped this mingling would also serve to cut down on sectional rivalries. *"Furthermore, a national university would keep so many young Americans from being sent abroad for an education, where they might lose their faith in republican institutions."*

Six pages of Washington's will are devoted to education. In it he made three separate bequests in regard to education. He had founded and in part supported the first free school in Virginia, the Alexandria Academy. This was mostly a charity school for orphaned and poor children. He had promiied the school Ł1,000 some years before but for some reason had paid Ł50 per year interest to the school rather than the sum itself. In his will he left $4,000 to this academy, which is no longer in existence.

He left fifty shares in the Potomac Company, which he had in turn received from the state of Virginia, to induce the federal government to establish a national university as he had been urging for some time. Congress did nothing to utilize this bequest, which was worth about Ł5,000, and the company later failed, thus completely negating the bequest.[78] He confirmed the gift of 100 shares of stock in the James River Company, which he had promised to Liberty Hall Academy. Liberty Hall in Lexington, Virginia, changed its name to Washington Academy to honor him and is now known as Washington and Lee University.[79] In a letter to the Academy trustees he said that: *"To promote literature in this rising empire and to encourage the arts have ever been among the warmest wishes of my heart."*

APPENDICES

After George Washington's death, an appraisal was made of the contents of each room of the mansion house, as required by law. One copy of this Appraiser's Inventory was filed at the Fairfax County court house, from which it disappeared during the Civil War. It later came into the possession of William K. Bixby, who gave it to the Mount Vernon Ladies' Association. An imperfect copy of the Appraiser's Inventory belonged to John A. Washington, last private owner of Mount Vernon, and was printed in Everett's **Life of George Washington** in 1860. All of these inventories are somewhat different. When Mrs. Washington died three years later, another inventory of Mount Vernon was made, and two different copies of it exist also. Appendices I and II are taken from **The Estate of George Washington, Deceased** by Eugene E. Prussing, who used the Bixby Inventory.

Appendix I
Inventory of Library Furnishings

In the Study
7 Swords & 1 blade $120
4 Canes 40
7 Guns 35
11 Spye Glasses 110
1 Tin canister drawg Paper   50
Trumbuls Prints 36
1 Case Surveyors Instrumts 10
1 Traveling Ink Case 3
1 Globe 5
1 box contg. 2 Paper moulds 25
1 Picture 3
1 Chest of Tools 15
1 Bureau 7
1 Dressg Table 40

(11)   1 Tambour Secretary 80
1 Walnut Table 5
1 Copying press 30
1 Compass-Staff & 2 Chairs 30
1 Old Copying press 11

1 Case Dentists Instrumts 10
2 Setts money weights 20
1 Telescope 50
1 Box Paints &c. 15
1 Bust of General Washington in
    plaister from the life 100
1 do. Marble 50
1 Profile in plaister 25
2 Seals with Ivory handles 8
1 Pocket Compass   50
1 Brass Level 10
1 Japan box containg a masons
    Apron 40
1 Small case containg 3 Straw rings⎫
1 Farmers Luncheon box   ⎬ . . . 1   75
1 Silk Sash (Military) 20
1 Velvet housing for a saddle &
    holsters trimmed with silver lace 5
1 Piece of Oil cloth contg orders of
    Masonry 50
Some Indian presents 5
2 Pine writing Tables 4
1 Circular Chair 20
1 Box Military figures 2
1 Brass model Cannon 15
2 Brass candlesticks 2
2 horse whips 4
1 pr Steel Pistols 50
1 Copper Wash bason   75
1 Chest & its contents (Gloves &c) . . . 100
1 Fan Chair 5 2
1 Writing Stand & apparatus 5
1 (Green) field Book   25
Balloon flag 1
Tongs Shovel & fender 1
A Painted likeness of Lawe W—n 10
1 Oval Looking Glass 2
3 pr Pistols 50

In the Iron Chest.

6 per cent., 3746	3746	
Stock of the U.S. Dr. Deferred, 1873	2500	6,246.00
3 per cent., 2946		
25 Shares Stock of the Bank of Alexandria,		5,000.00
24 do. do. Potomac Company, (at L100 st'g.)		
		10.666.00
Cash,		254.70
1 Sett of Shoe and Knee Buckles, Paste, in Gold,		250.00
1 Pair of Shoe and Knee Buckles, Silver,		5.00
2 Gold Cincinnati Eagles,		30.00
1 Diamond do.		387.00
1 Gold Watch, Chain, two Seals, and a Key,		175.00
1 Compass in Brass Case,		.50
1 Gold Box, Presented by the Corporation of New New York,		100.00
5 Shares of James River Stock at $100,		500.00
170 Shares of Columbia Stock at $40,		$6,800.00
1 Large Gold Medal of General Washington,		150.00
1 Gold Medal of St. Patrick's Society,		8.00
1 Ancient Medal (another Metal,)		2.00
11 Medals in a Case,		50.00
1 Large Medal of Paul Jones,		4.00
3 Other Metal Medals,		1.00
1 Brass Engraving of the Arms of the United States,		10.00
1 Pocket Compass,		5.00
1 Case of Instruments, Parallel Rule, &c.		17.50
1 Pocket Book,		5.00

Appendix II
Inventory of Books

	Vs.		D.	C.
(13) Library				
Case No. 1				
American Encyclopaedia	18	4to	150	
Skambeaud Dictionary	1	"	7	50
Memoir of a map. Hindostan	1	"	8	
Young's Travels	1	"	4	
Johnsons Dictionary	2	"	10	
Gutheries Geography	2	"	20	
Elements of Riging	2	"	20	
Principles of taxation	1	"	2	
Luzac's Oration	1	"	1	
Mawes Gardner	1	"	4	
Geofreys Aerial Voyage	1	"	1	
Beacon Hill	1	"	1	
Memoirs of the American Academy				
(one of which is a pamphlet).......	2	"	3	
Du Hamels husbandry	1	"	2	
Langley on Gardening..............	1	4to	2	
Price's Carpenter	1	"	1	
Count de Grace	1	"	1	
Miller's Gardners Dictionary	1	"	5	
Gibsons diseases of horses	1	"	3	
Rumfords Essays			3	
Millers Tracts	1	8vo	2	
Rowleys works....................	4	"	12	
Robertsons Charles the 5th	4	"	16	
Gordons history of America.........	4	"	12	
Gibbons Roman Empire	6	"	18	
Stanyans Grecian history	2	"	2	
Adams's Rome	2	"	4	
Andersons Institute	1	"	2	
Robertsons America	2	"	4	
Genl Washingtons letters	2	"	4	
Ossian's Poems	1	"	2	
Humphrey's works	1	"	3	
King of Prussia's works	13	"	26	
(14) Gillies Frederick	1	"	1	50
Goldsmiths natural history..........	8	"	12	
Locke on Understanding	2	"	3	
Shiply's Works....................	2	"	4	
Buffon's natural history abridged	2	"	4	
Ramsay's history	2	"	2	

Title	Qty	Format		
The Bee the 13th vl missing	18	"	34	
Sullies memoirs	6	"	9	
Fletchers Apeal	1	"	1	
History of Spain	2	"	3	
Porteus Sermons	2	"	2	
Chapman on education	1	"		75
Smiths wealth of nations	3	"	4	50
History of Louisiana	2	"	2	
Warrens Poems	1	"		50
Junius's Letters	1	"	1	
City Addresses	1	"	1	
Conquest of Canaan	1	"	1	
Shakespears Works	1	"	2	
Antidotes to Deism	2	"	1	
Memoirs of 2500	1	"		75
			445	50

In Case No. 2

Title	Qty	Format		
Forests Voyage	1	4to	3	
Don Quixote	4	"	12	
Furgusons Roman History	3	"	12	
Watsons History of Philip 3rd	1	4to	4	
Barklays Apology	1	"	3	
Uniform of the forses of Great Britain in 1742	1	"	20	
Otways Art of War	1	"	3	
Political State of Europe	8	8vo	20	
Winchesters Lectures	4	"	6	
Principles of Hydrolics	2	"	2	
(15) Leigh on Opium	1	"		75
Heth's memoirs	1	"	2	
American Museum	10	"	15	
Vertots Rome	2	"	2	
Hartes Gustavus	2	"	2	
Moores Navigation	1	"	2	
Graham on Education	1	"	2	
History of the Mission among the Indians in No. America	1	"	2	
French Constitution	1	"	1	50
Wyntrops Journal	1	"	1	50
American Magazine	2	"	4	
Watts's Views	1	4to	20	
History of Marshall Turenne	2	8vo	2	
Ramsays Revolution of So Carolina	2	"	2	

History of Quadrupeds	1	"	1	50
Carvers Travels	1	"	1	50
Moores Italy	2	"	3	
Do. France	2	"	3	
Chastelleaux Travels	1	"	1	
Chareloix Voyage	1	"	1	
Volneys Travels	2	"	3	
Ditto Ruins	1	"	1	50
Warvills voyage in French	3	"	3	
Warvills in the relation of France & the U.S.			1	
			607	75

No. 3

Miscellanies	1	4to	1	
Fulton on Small Canals & Iron Bridges	1	"	3	
Liberty a Poem	1	"		50
Hazards collection of State Papers	2	"	5	
Youngs Travels	2	"	4	
Wests Discourse	1	"	2	

(16)	A State of the Representation of England & Wales	1	4to		50
	Miscellanies	2	"	2	
	Political Pieces	1	"	1	
	Treaties	1	"		50
	Annual Register for 1781	1	8vo		75
	Masonic Constitution	1	4to	1	
	Smiths do.	1	"		50
	Prestons Poems	2	"	1	
	History of the U.S. 1796	1	8vo		50
	Parliamentory debates	12	"	6	
	Mairs Book-keeping	1	"	1	50
	Parliamentory Debates	1	"		50
	Plays Mrs. Lewis's	1	"		
	Miscellanies	1	"	1	
	Proceedings of the E. India Compy	1	fol	4	
	Ladies Magazine (Taken by Bushd Washington)	2	8vo	3	
	Parliamentory Register	7	"	3	50
	Pryors documents	2	"	2	
	Remembraucer	6	"	3	
	European Magazine	2	"	3	
	Columbian ditto	5	"	10	

Title	Qty	Size		
American do. (taken by Judge Wn)	1	"	2	
New York do.	1	"	2	
Christians do.	1	"	2	
Walker on Magnetism	1	"		50
Monroe's view of the Executive	1	"		75
Massechusets Magazine (takn by Judge W—n)	2	"	4	
A 5 Minutes Ansr. to Paynes letter to Genl. W—n	1	"	1	
Political Tracts	1	"	2	
Proceedings on Parliamentory Reform	1	"	2	
Poems on Various Subjects	1	"		50
Plays &c	1	"		75
Annual Register	3	"	4	50
Botanico Medical disertation	1	"		25
Oracle of Liberty	1	"		25
(17) Cadmus	1	"	1	
Doctrine of projectiles	1	"		50
Patricus the Utilist	1	"		50
Ahymen Rezon	1	"	1	50
Sharp on Prophecies	1	"		75
Minto on Planets	1	"		50
Sharp on the English Tongue	1	8vo		50
Do. on limitation of Slavery	1	"	1	50
Do. on the Peoples rights	1	"	1	
Do. Remarks	1	"		50
National defence	1	"		50
Sharps free Military	1	"		50
Do. on Congressional Courts &c	1	"		75
Ahymen Rezon	1	"	1	
Vision of Columbus, 2 Setts	1	"		50
Wilsons Lectures	1	"		75
Miscellanies	1	"	1	
The Contrast a Comedy	1	"		75
Sharp an appendix on Slavery	1	"		50
Muirs tryal	1	"		75
End of Time	1	"		75
Erskins view of the War	1	"	1	
Political Magazine	3	"	4	50
The law of Nature	1	12mo		75
Washingtons legacy	1	"	1	
Political Tracts	1	8vo	1	
America	1	"	1	
Proof of a Conspiracy	1	"	1	50
Mackintosh's defence	1	"	1	

Miscellanies 1	"	1	
Mirabeau 1	"	1	
Virginia Journal 1	4to	1	
Miscellanies 1	8vo	1	25
Poems &c 1	4to	1	
Morses Geography 1	8vo	2	
Messages &c 1	"	1	
History of Ireland 2	"	2	
Hartes Works 1	"	1	25
Political Pamphlet 1	"	1	
Burnes's Poems 1	"	2	

18)	Political Tracts 1	"		75
	Miscellanies 1	"	1	
	Higgans on Cements 1	"	1	
	Repository 2	"	3	
	Reign of George the 3d 1	"	1	
	Political Tracts 1	"	1	25
	Tar Water 1	"		75
	Minots History 1	"		75
	Mease on the bite of a Mad dog 1	"		75
	Political Tracts 1	"	1	
	Reports 1	"	1	
	Revolution of France 1	8vo	1	
	Essay on Property 1	"	1	
	Sir Henry Clintons narrative 1	"	1	
	Lord Norths Administration 1	"	1	50
	Lloyds Rhapsody 1	"	1	
	Tracts 1	"	1	
	Inland Navigation 1	"	1	
	Chesterfield letters 1	"	1	50
	Smiths Constitution 1	4to	1	
	Morses Geography 2	8vo	4	
	Belknaps American Biography (taken			
	out by Judge W—n) 2	"	3	
	Do. History of New hampshire 1	''	2	
	Do. Do........................... 3	"	5	
	Minots History of Massachusetts 1	"	2	
	Jenkinsons collection of Treaties 3	"	6	
	District of Maine 1	"	1	50
	Gullivers Travels 2	"	1	50
	Tracts on Slavery.................. 1	"	1	
	Priestleys evidences 1	"	1	
	Life of Buncle 2	"	3	
	Websters Essays 1	"	1	50
	Bartrans Travels (taken out by			
	Judge W—n) 1	"	2	

Bossu's do.	2	"	3	
Situation of America	1	"	1	
Jeffersons Notes	1	"	1	50

(19)	Coxes view	1	"	1	50
	Ossians Poems (Mrs. W—ns)	1	"	1	50
	Adams on Globes	1	"	2	
	Pikes Arithmetic	1	"	2	
	Banaby's Sermons & Travels	1	"	1	
	Champion on Commerce	1	"	1	
				804	

No. 5

Browns Bible	1	fol	15	
Bishop Wilsons ditto	3	"	60	
Ditto do. works	1	"	15	
Laws of New York	2	"	12	
Do. of Virginia	2	"	3	
Middletons Architecture	1	"	3	
Millers naval ditto	1	"	4	
The Senators Remembrancer	1	"	3	
The Origin of the Tribes of Nations in America	1	8vo		75
A Treatise on the principles of Commerce between Nations	1	8vo		50
Annual Register	1	"		50
Genl Washingtons Letters	2	"	4	
Insurrection	1	"		50
American Remembrancer	3	"	1	50
Epistles for the ladies	1	"		50
Discourses upon Common Prayer	1	"		25
The tryal of the 7 Bishops	1	"		50
Lebaines Surveyor	1	fol	1	

(21)	Sharp on the law of Nature	1	"		25
	Do. on the law of Retribution	1	"		25
	On Libels and Juries	1	"		25
	Acts of Congress	1	"		75
	Debates of the Convention of Virga	1	"		50
	The Landlords law	1	12mo		25
				25	
	Attorneys Pocket Book	2	8vo	1	
	Presidents Messages	1	"	2	
	Jays Treaty	1	"		50
	Debates of the Convention of Massechuts	1	"		50

Law against Bankrupts	1	"		50
Debates in the Convention of Pennsylvania	1	"		50
Do. in Virginia	1	"		50
Do. in the house of Representatives of the United States with respect to their power on Treaties	1	"		50
Sundry Pamphlets containing messages from the President to Congress &c &c &c &c			1	
			1,120	25
No. 7				
Orations	1	4to		50
Original and present State of man	1	8vo		50
Gospel News	1	"	1	
Mosaical Oration	1			75
Sermons	2	"	1	50
Political ditto	3	"	2	25
Miscellanies	1	"		75
Ray on the wisdom of God in Creation	1	"	1	
Orations	1	"		75
Medical Tracts	2	"	1	50
Masonic Sermons	1	"		50
Miscellanies	1	"		75
Backus's history	1	"	1	
Sick Man visited	1	"		75
State of Man	1	"		75
Churchils Sermon	1	"		75
Account of the Protestant Church	1	"		75
Exposition of the 39 Articles	1	"	1	
Dodington's diary	1	"	1	
Davies Cavalry	1	"	1	
Simons military course	1	"	1	
(22) Gentelmens magazine	3	"	4	50
Library Catalogue	1	"	1	50
Transactions of the royal humane Society	1	"	3	
Zimmermans Survey	1	"		75
History of Barbara	1	"		75
Ansons voyage round the world	1	"	1	
Horseman and farrier	1	"	1	
Gordons Geography	1	"	1	
Kentucky	1	"		75
History of Virginia	1	"	1	
American Revolution	1	"	1	

Cincinnati 1	"	1	
Political Tracts 1	"		75
Remarks on the encroachment of the			
River Thames 1	"		50
Sharp on Crown law 1	"		50
Common Sense &c 1	"		75
Hardy's Tablet 1	"		75
Beauties of Sterne 1	"		75
Peregrin Pickle 3	"	1	50
Mc Fingal 1	"		50
Memoirs of the noted Buckhorse 2	"	1	
Sharps Sermons 1	8vo		50
Muirs discourse 1	"		75
Emblems Divine & Moral 1	"	1	
Yoricks Sermons 2	"	1	
D' Ivornois on Agriculture, Colonies			
and Commec 1	"		75
Pocket Dictionary 1	"		25
Prayer Book (Mrs. W—ns) 1	"	1	50
Royal English Grammar 1	"		25
Principles of Trade Compared 1	"		50
Dr. Morses Sermon 1	"		50
Duche's Sermon, 1775 1	"		50
(20) Sermons 1	"		50
Hales contemplations moral and divine 1	"		50
Sermons 1	"		75
Embassy to China 1	"	1	
Warrens Poems 1	"	1	
Sermons 1	"		25
Humphrey Clinker 1	"		25
Poems 1	"		50
Swifts Works .1	"		50
History of a foundling (3d wanting) . . .3	"	1	50
Adventures of Telemachus 2	"	2	
Nature displayed 1	"	1	
Solyman and Almenia 1	"		50
Plays 1	"		50
The high German Doctor 1	"		25
Benezets Discourse 1	"		25
Life and Death of the Earl of			
Rochester 1	"		25
		948	00

No. 6
Journals of the Senate and House of
Represts . . . . .9 fol   27

Title	Qty	Format		
Laws of the U. States	7	fol	28	
Revised Laws of Virginia	1	"	10	
Acts of Virginia Assembly	5	"	1	
Crutwells concordance	1	"	5	
Dallas's Reports	1	8vo	3	
Swifts System	2	"	3	
Journals of the Senate and house of Represts	3	"	6	
State Papers	1	"	2	
Burn's Justice	4	"	12	
Martins law of Nations	1	"	1	50
View of the British Customs	1	"	1	
Debates of Congress	3	"	4	50
Journals of do.	13	"	40	
Laws of the United States	3	"	6	
Kirbys Reports	1	"	2	
Virginia Justice	1	"	1	
Do. Laws	1	"	1	
Dogge of Criminal Law	3	"	4	50
Laws of the U. States	2	"	4	
Debates of the State of Massechusets on the Constitution	1	"		50
Odyssey (Pope of Homer)	5	8vo	3	
Miscellanies	1	"	1	50
Indostian Letters[6]	1	vol		50
Voltairs' do.[6]	1	vol		50
Guardian[6]	2	"	1	
Beauties of Swift[6]	1	"		50
The Gleener[6]	3	"	3	
Miscelanies[6]	2	"	1	50
Lee's Memoirs	1	8vo	1	
The Universalist	1	"	1	
Chesterfield letters	4	"	2	
Louis the 15th	4	"	3	
Panopticon	3	"	2	
Reason &c	1	"		50
Tour thro' Great Britain	4	"	3	
Female fortune hunter	3	"	1	
The supposed daughter	3	"	1	50
Gillblass	4	"	3	
Columbian Grammar	1	"		50
Frasers assistant	1	"		50
Review of Cromwells life	1	"		75
Seneca's morals	1	"		75
Travels of Cyrus	1	"		75
Miscellanies	1	"		75

Charles the 12th	1	"		50
Emma Corbet (the 2d wantg)	2	"	1	

(23)	Popes works	6	12mo		2
	Foresters	1	"		50
	Adams's defence	1	8vo		75
	Butlers Hudibras	1	"	1	
	Spectator	6	"	3	
	New Crusoe	1	"		75

1,200	25

No. 8

Philadelphia Gazette	1	fol	10
Pennsylvania Packet	2	"	12
Gazette of the U. States	10	"	40
Atlas to Gutheries Grammar	1	"	
Molls atlas	1	"	10
West India do.	1	"	20
Genl Kotographer	1	"	30
Atlas of No America	1	"	10
Manoeuvres	1	8vo	1

6These six items were inserted in the margin in writing of Lear.

Military Instructions	1	8vo		50
Count Saxe's plan for new modeling the french Army	1	"		50
Military disciplin	1	4to	2	
Prussian evolutions	1	"	1	50
Code of Military Standing Resolutions	2	"	4	
Field Engineer	1	8vo	1	50
Army list	1	"		75
Prussian Evolutions	1	4to	2	
Leblonds Engineer	2	8vo	3	
Muller on fortifications	1	"	2	
Essay on field Artillery by Anderson	1	"		75
A System of Camp discription	1	"	2	
Essay on the Art of War	1	"	1	
Treatise by Blaine of Military disciplin	1	"	1	50
List of Military officers British & Irish in 1777	1	"		50
Vallance on fortification	1	"	1	50
Muller on Artillery	1	"	1	50
Do. on fortification	1	"	2	
Militia	1	"	1	
American Atlas	1	fol	4	

Stubends regulation	1 8vo		75
Traite cavileer	1 fol	6	

(24)

Truxton on Latitude &c. &c.	1 "	1	50
Ordinances of the King	1 "	2	
Magnetic Atlas	1 "	1	
Roads thro' England	1 8vo	1	
Carey's War Atlas	1 fol		75
Collis's Survey of Roads	1 8vo		50
Military Institutions for Officers	1 "		50
Norfolk Exercise	1 "		25
Advice of Officers of the British Army	1 "		25
Webbs Treatise on the appointmts of the army	1 "		25
Acts of Parliament respectg militia	1 "		25
The Partizan	1 "		50
Anderson on Artillery in French	1 "		25
List of Officers under Sr. Wm. Howe in America	1 "		25
The Military Guide	1 "		50
The duties of Soldiers in General	3 "	1	50
		1,384	75

On the Table

Youngs Tour	2 8vo	3	
Do. on Agriculture	26 "		
Note. 17 vos. full bound, 8 half and 1 pamphlet		50	
Anderson on Agriculture (1 vol. full bound, the others in boards)	4 "	8	
Lisles observations on husbandry	2 "	3	
Museum Rusticum	6 "	10	
Marshalls rural ornament	2 "	4	
Barlows husbandry	2 "	3	
Kennedy on Gardening	2 "	2	
Hale on husbandry	4 "	6	
Sentimental Magazine	5 "	10	
Price on the Picturesque	2 "	4	
Agriculture	2 "	2	
Millers Gardners Calendar	1 "	2	
Rural Œconomy	1 "	1	
Agricultural enquiries	1 "	1	
Maxwells practical husbandry	1 "	2	
Boswell on Meadows	1 "	1	
Gentlemans Farmer	1 "	1	50
Practical Do.	1 "	1	50

(25)	Millwright and Millers guide 1	"	2	
	Bordley on husbandry 1	"	2	25
	Sketches and Enquiries 1	"	2	
	Farmers Complete guide 1	"	1	
	The Solitary or Cathusian Gardner 1	"	1	
	Homers Illiad by Pope (first and secd. wanting) 4	"	2	
	Donquixote 4	"	3	
	Federalist 2	"	3	
	The world displayed (the 13th wantg) . 19	12mo	9	50
	Searches Essays 2	8vo	2	
	Freneaus Poems 1	"	1	
	Cattle Doctor 1	"		75
	Steven's Directory 1	"		50
	New System of Agriculture 1	"		50
	Columbus's discovery 1	"		25
	Moores Travels 5	"	4	
	Agricultural Society of New York 1	4to	2	
	Transactions of ditto 1	"	1	
	Annals of Agriculture 1	"	2	
	Dundonnales connection between Agriculture and Chymestry 1	"	1	
	Labours in husbandry 1	4to	1	
	Acct. of different Kinds of Sheep 1	8vo		50
	The hot house Gardner 1	"	1	50
	Historical Memoirs of Frederick the 2d 3	"	1	
	Treatise of Peat Moss 1	"		50
	Do. on bogs and swampy grounds 1	"		75
	Compleat Farmer 1	fol	6	
			1,551	75
	Pamphlets in No. 1			
	Reports of the national Agricultural Society of Great Britain 100	4to	25	
	Massechusets Magazine 41	8vo	6	
	New York do. 38	"	6	
	London do. 18	"	3	
(26)	Political Magazine 8	"	1	
	Universal Assylum 9	"	1	50
	Do. Magazine 11	"	1	50
	Country do. 15	"	2	
	Monthly and Critical Reviews 11	"	2	
	Gentlemans Magazine 8	"	1	
	Congressional Register 9	"	1	
	Miscellaneous Magazine 27	"	3	
	Tom Paynes Rights of Man 43	"	15	

No. 2
 Miscellanious Magazine . . . . .27 " 4

Books in Lower Part of No. 3
 Hazards collection of State papers . . . . .2 fol 5 taken out
 Morses American Gaziteer 1 8vo 2
 Annals of Agriculture (No. 20 & 21) . . .2 " 3 do.
 Boucher on the American Revolu-
  tion 1 8vo 1 50
 15 Pamphlets Annals of Agriculture . . . 2 50
 Judge Peters on Plaster of Paris 3
  setts (1 taken out). . . . . .1 " 1 50
 Belknaps Biography . . . . .1 " 1 50
 American Remembrancer . . . . .1 " 50
 Federalist . . . . .2 " 1 50
 A Pamphlet the debates of Parliament
  on the articles of Peace . . . . .1 " 25
 History of the American War in 17
  Pamphlets. 1 50
 Miscellaneous Pamphlets 20 8vo 2
 Washington a Poem 9 Setts (2 out) 2
 A manuscript on finance 1
 Bruto Primo an Italian Tragedy . . . . . . .1 " 1
(27) Fragment of Politics and literature
  by Mandrillion in French . . . . .1 " 75
 Revolutions of France and Geneva do. .2 " 2
 History of the Administration of the
  finances of the french Republic . . . . .1 " 50
 History of the french administration . . .1 " 75
 The social compact in french . . . . .1 " 25
 Chattelleaux travels in N. America do .2 " 1 50
 1 Pamphlet of the french Revolution
  at Geneva 25
 America delivered a Poem in french . . .2 " 1 50
 Sinclairs Statystics do. . . . . .1 " 1
 The works of Monsieur Chamouset do. 2 " 4
 Letters of an American farmer do. . . . . .3 " 4 50
 Germanichus do. . . . . .1 " 25
 Triumph of the New World do. . . . . . . .2 " 1 50
 United States of America in German . . .1 " 1 50
 Abbe Rynals discourse on the advan-
  tage of the discovery of America . . . .1 " 1
 A German Book . . . . .1 " 25
 The french murcury in french. . . . . . . .4 " 3
 Essay on weight, measure &c . . . . .2 " 75
 History of England . . . . .2 " 25

Political Journal in German 1   "   50
Letters in french and English do 1   "   25
A disertation on the Bragans of Silks
    do. 1   "   50
History of the holy Scripture do 1   "   25
Do. of Gillblass do. 2   "   1
Telemachus do. 2   "   1
Poems of M. Grecourt do. 2   "   25
Court Register in English 6 12mo   1   50
6 pamphlets, Political Jou(r)nal in
    German   50

In No. 5

Description of a monument 1   "   50
Beacon Hill 1   "   25
Letters on the English and German
    language 1   "   25
A family house keeper 1   "   25
Pamphlets of different discriptions   15

(28) Maps Charts &c.

Chart of the Navigation from the Gulph of
    Florida to Philada. (by Hamilton Moore)
    and from do. to Funday Bay . . . . :40
Howells large Map of Pennsylvania 10
Griffiths Map of Maryland and 10
    Sketch of Delaware. 8
Henry's Map of Virginia 8
Bradley's do. of the United States 5
Holland's do. of Newhamshire 3
Ellicots Map of the west end of lake Ontario 4
Hutchins Map of the western part of Virginia,
    Pennsylvania, Maryland and North Carolina . . .3
Adlum and Wallaces Map of Pennsylvania 2
Map of Kennebec River & ca. 1
Andrews, Military Map of the seat of War in the
    Netherlands 1
Howells small Map of Pennsylvania 2
Great Canal between Forth and Clide 2
Plan of the line between North Carolina and
    Virginia 2
McMurrays Map of the United States 3
Military plans of the American Revolution 8
Evans's map of Pennsylvania, New Jersey New
    York and Delaware. 1
Plan of the Mississippe from the River Iverville
    to the River Yazous 2

Maps of India 5
Sundry Plans of Federal City and District . . . . —
Chart of France 1
Maps of the World 50
Map of the State of Connecticut 2
Spanish Maps 50

(29) Map of Holland 1
Table of Commerce and Population of France 50
Battle of the Nile, &c. 1
Routs and order of Battle Genl Sinclair and
    Harmer 1
Truxton on the rigging of a Frigate 1
View of the encampment of West Point 50
Emblematic Prints by Dr. Buxton 4
Prints of Washington and la Fayette . . . . —
Plan of the Government house of New York 50
Chase and action between the Constellation and
    Insurgeant 2 prints 4
Genl. Wilkinsons Map of Part of the Western
    Territory 1
Plan of Mt. Vernon by Jno. Vaughan 1
Specimen of Penmanship 50
Plans of the Federal City and District 5
1 Large Dft 3
Plan of the City of New York, Panocticon 50
Hoops Map of the State of New York 1
Howells Pocket Map of the State of Pennsa 2
French Map of the Carolina's 2
Fry and Jeffersons Map of Virginia 2
Howells Small map of Pennsylvania 2
A map of New England 2

(30) 9 Maps of different parts of Virginia and Caro-
    lina and a number of loose maps and Charts,
    &c. &c. 52
Carltons Map (2 Setts) of the Coasts of North
    America 8
Treatise on Cavalry with large Cuts 50
Walkers view in Scotland 3
A large Port folio with sundry engras 40
Alexanders Victories and 6 prints 100
8 Reames large folio Paper 40
2 do. small do. 8
13 do. letter do. 39
5 Whole Packages Sealing Wax 5
5 leaden Paper presses . . . . —
6 Blank Books 18

13 do. Small............................2		
1 large Globe 50		
1 Trunk 6		
	2,266	

Books Omitted.

Dictionary of Arts and Sciences.......4 8vo	20	
Smolletts History of England ....11 "	11	
Handmaid to the Arts	2	
Bencrofft on permanent colors........1 "	1	
One Theodolite	50	

(31) In the Closet under Franks direction

24 China Dishes	15	
2 " butter boats		25
20 " deep plates	3	
48 " shallow do................	8	

APPENDIX III

Library of Colonel Augustine Washington

(*Westmoreland Inventories,* Book 4, page 178)*

"Inventory of Colonel Augustine Washington Dec'd: (abstracts only therefrom) . . .

In the library:

13 Volumes of Rapin's History of England
9 Volumes of The Spectator
2 Volumes of The Guardian
3 Volumes of Virgils
6 Volumes of Pope's Homer
2 Volumes of Abridgment of the Reformation
6 Volumes of Clarendon's History of the Rebellion
1 Webb's Ving^a Justice
1 Great Lexicon
2 Volumes of Conquest of Mexico
3 Volumes of Magazines
8 Volumes of Clark's Sermons
6 Volumes of Shakespeare's Plays
Gordon's Geographical Grammar
Art of Cookery
1 Large Bible
1 Large Common Prayer Book
Sundry old English & Latin books (titles not given)

*From: *Tyler's Quarterly Historical and Geneological Magazine,* Vol. 8, No. 2, p. 92.

APPENDIX IV

Catalogue of the Library of Daniel Parke Custis

From a Manuscript in the Collection of the
Virginia Historical Society.*

(Daniel Park Custis, of "The White House," New Kent Co.,
Virginia, and of Williamsburg, died in 1757, leaving a widow,
Martha, who married on January 6, 1759, George Washington,
and one son, John Parke Custis. The catalogue here printed was
no doubt made soon after the marriage of Mrs. Custis to Col.
Washington, and as the initials indicate, a partial division of the
books had been made, some going to Washington in right of his
wife, and others set aside for young Custis, then only a child of six
years. No doubt some of the books had been inherited by D. P.
Custis from his father, Hon. John Custis.)

Catesby's N'l H'y, 2 v. ....J. C.
English Atlas, 1 ....Do.
Maps, Do, 1 ....G. W.
2d Vol. of Chamb'rs D'y ....Do.
Virg'a Laws...............................G. W. & J. C.
Salmon's H'y Plants ....J. C.
Fuller's History English Worthys...................J. C.
Bonner's Guide to ye Great Physician ....Do.
Aesop's Fables by S'r Roger le Estrange ....J. C.
Ditto   Ditto   Ditto ....G. W.
Mons'r De Thevenet's Travels to the Levant ....J. C.
Brown's Travels ....Do.
Dalton's Justice ....Do.
2 Bibles, 1 J. C. & 1 G. W.
Gibson's Farriery ....G. W.
Duhamel's Husb'y ....Do.
Langley's Garden's ....Do.
Shaw's Chemistry ....J. C.
Power of Drugs.................................Do.
Plays by Sundry Hands ....Do.
Lee's Plays ....Do.
Plays by Sundry Hands ....Do.
Markham's Far'y...............................Do.
Gent'n Journal.................................Do.
Harvey's Philosophy ....Do.
Merchants Magazine ....Do.
Brady's Sermons ....Do.
Parisonus.....................................Do.
Dodsley's An'l Register, 4 v. ....G. W.

Smollet's H'y of England, 4 Do. .Do.
Haly Husbandry 4 Do. . . . . .Do.
Lisles Do. 2 Do. . . . . .Do.
Farmer's Guide . . . . .Do.
Maxwell's H'y . . . . .Do.
Mercer's Abridgment . . . . .Do.
Salleysch's Farriery . . . . .Do.
Life of Mahomet . . . . .Do.
Brown's Enquiry into Vulgar Errors . . . . .J. C.
Cowley's Works . . . . .Do.
Leybourn's Survey . . . . .G. W.
Debates Parl't, 12 Vol. . . . . .J. C.
Clarendon's H'y Reb'n, 7 v. . . . . .J. C.
Theory of ye Earth, 2 . . . . .J. C.
Gullivers Travels, 2 . . . . .Do.
Excise Bih (?) . . . . .Do.
No. Excise, 2 v. . . . . .Do.
Barcley's Apology . . . . .Do.
Political State of G. B., 5 Vols., 2 Wanting . . . . .J. C.
Shaw's P. Physick, 2 . . . . .J. C.
London Spy, 4, 2 Wanting . . . . .Do.
Crusoe, 3 . . . . .Do.
Voyage R'd ye World . . . . .Do.
Salman's Dictionary . . . . .Do.
Do. Dispens'y . . . . .Do.
Do. Praxis Medica . . . . .Do.
Echard's R. Hist'y . . . . .Do.
Dryden's Juvenal . . . . .Do.
Do. Miscell'us Poems, 2 Vols .Do.
Dampier's Voyages, 4 . . . . .Do.
Buckaneers of Amer. . . . . .Do.
Anson's Voyage . . . . .G. W.
Annals of King G. . . . . .J. C.
Revolution Politicks . . . . .Do.
Cromwell's Life . . . . .Do.
Gentleman Instructed . . . . .Do.
Baytive Practice Phys'k . . . . .Do.
Lobb on the Stone . . . . .Do.
Tuker's Prescrip'n . . . . .Do.
Turner on ye Skin . . . . .Do.
Mandevilles Dialogues . . . . .Do.
Wiseman's Survery, 2 v. . . . . .Do.
Estmallen's (?) Abridg't . . . . .Do.
Cockl'n (?) of a Garosse (?) . . . . .Do.
Drake's Anatomy, 2 . . . . .Do.
Quincey's Eng. Disp'y . . . . .Do.

Sydenham Work . . . . Do.
Dictionarium Rusticum . . . . Do.
Cum on ye Venereal Dis. . . . . Do.
Bulstrode's Essays . . . . Do.
Paxton's Essays . . . . Do.
Cockburn on Fluxes . . . . J. C.
Hoadley on the Sacrament . . . . Do.
Gibson's Farriers disp'y . . . . Do.
Bland Mili'y Discp'n . . . . G. W.
Terence in English . . . . J. C.
Epistles for Ladies . . . . G. W.
King's State of ye Protest'ns Ireland . . . . Do.
Drake's Historia Angli Scotica . . . . J. C.
Chamberlayne on ye old Test . . . . J. C.
Spectulatis 2 . . . . J. C.
Hippocrates Aphorisms . . . . J. C.
Letters of Wit & Politicks . . . . J. C.
Memors of Lord Holles . . . . J. C.
Foster's Sermons . . . . J. C.
Blair's Sermons . . . . Do.
Parkes Administration . . . . Do.
Cheyne of Health.
Essay of Fevers.
Ovids Epistles.
Sick Man Visited.
Collier of ye Stage.
Turner of Gleets.
Waller's Poems.
Welwood's Memoirs.
Bacon's Essays.
Journey thro' China.
Wainewright of ye Non-Natu'n.
Duty of Man.
Don Quixot 4 Vols.
Cato's Letters 4 Do.
Plutarch's Morals 5 Do.
Guardian 2 Do.
    Do. 2 Do.
Independent Whig 3 Do.
Craftsman 14 Do.
Turkish Spy 9.
Paradise Lost.
Perigrine Pickle 3.
Tatlers 4 Vols.
Tour thro' G. Brit. 4.
Compl't Tradesman 2.

Free thinker 3 Vols.
Pope's Works 3.
      Do.   Do. 1st wanting 4.
Swifts Micellaneous, 2 & 5 Vols. want'g, 4.
Spectators 5 Vol. want'g, 7.
Spectators 7 & 8 want'g, 6.
Buckhorse 2 (erased).
Feamale Fortune H'r 3.
Foundling 4.
Dissertation on ye Mosaic.
Ray's Wisdom of God.
Compleat View British Customs.
Gordon's Geo. (?) Grammer.
Canber on ye Com'n Prayer.
Sportsmans Dictionary.
Trial of ye Seven Bishops.
Vaubans Fortifications (erased).
Wagstafs Works.
Jones of Opium.
White on Fevers.
Josephus Epitomis'd.
Taylor's Holy Living.
Sir Walter Rawleigh's H'y of ye World.
State Poems, 2 Vols. missing.
Voyage to the Levant.
South's Sermons, 1 & 2 missing, 3 Vol.
State Poems by Sundry h'ds.
Thoughts on Religion 3 vols.
Sermons.
Dryden's Juvenal.
Watton's Reflections.
Martiall's Epigrams.
Bishop of Bath's Sermons.
Charge to Grand Jury.
Collier Answered 4 Books.
Miller's Gard'rs Dict'y.
Dryden's Mis'y Poems 2 Books.
Miscel'a Poems.
Behns Poems.
Art of Contentm't.
Government of ye Tongue.
Gentlemans Calling.
Ladies Calling.
Lively Oracles.
Revolution of Sweden.
English Dict'y.

Firmeu's Life.
Fashions and entertainm't.
Ovid's Travels.
Hist'y of ye Piratical Sta.
Desolation of France.
Roman Antiquities.
Works of King Chas. 1st.
Conjugal Lewdness.
Oldham's Works.
Echard's Gazetteer.
Poligraphica.
Wits com'n Wealth.
Heathen Gods.
Scaron's Novels.
Seneca's Morals.
Bate's Dispensatory.
Plutarchs Lives, 5 Vols.
Salm'ns Synopsis Medicina.
Dike Saplusium (?).
Willis Practice Physick.
Lives of ye 12 Caesars.
English Parnassus.
Quintillian's Declamations.
Milton's Defence.
Pliny's Panegirick.
Notes on Dryden's Virgil.
Gould's Poems.
Creeche's Homer.
        Do. Lucretius.
Rochester's Letters, 2d Vol.
Winter Even'g Conf'nce.
Tate's Poems.
Miscellany Poems.
Pitt of Physick.
Jones de pebrifuge.
Government of a Wife.
Cole's English Dict'y.
London Dispensatory.
Echards Cond'ns on ye contempt of ye Clergy.
Docter Scarrified.
Ospring on Revel'n, Sermon.
Wingate's Arithmetick.
Parthenissa.
Sir M. Hales Contemp'n.
David Ranger 2 Vols.
Buckhorse 2 Do.

Telemechus 2 Do.
Seneca's Morals by way of Ar.
Travels of Cyrus.
Brown's Work's, 1, 2, 4 & 4 Vols.
Tryals at ye old Bailey.
Lord Landsdown's Works.
Atalantis 4 Vol.
Freeholder.
Yorrick's Sermons.
Bracken's Farriery.
Bawyers Hospt. Dispens'y.
Miltons Poems 2 V.
    Do. Paradise lost.
    Do. Regained.
    Do. Poems.
Hudibras.
Human Judgement.
Amours of ye F'h Kings.
State of England.
Locke of Education.
Religio Medici.
Osborne's Miscel.
Priests & Nuns.
Nature Display'd 2d Vol.
Some Passages of ye life & Death of ye E. Rochester.
Feamale Grievances.
Amours of ye K. of Tamona.
Pleasures of Matrimony.
Church Catechism expl'd.
Harris enq'y into ye Dis's Children.
Character of a Trimmer.
a little Vocabulary Latin & English.
Ovid's Tristia.
Phisical and Chemical Works.
An Apology of Human R.
A Poem in Hon'r of Tob'o.
Flowers & Plants.
The Court of St. German's or Sec't H'y of K'g James &
    Q'n Mary.
A Comp'n between ye Eloquence of Demosthenes & Cicero.
Academy of Eloquence.
The Game Law.
Brown's Eng'h Gram'r or Spel.
The Family Physician.
Advice to a Son.
Help & Guide to Ch'n Fam.
Flower Garden & Vineyard.

Cocker's Arithmetick.
Laws Con'g Landlord & Ten't.
Treatise of ye Diseases of Inf. & children.
Vaughan's Poems.
Wits Commonwealth.
The honest man or art to please in Court.
English liberties.
Hodder's Arithmetick.
The hist'y of Justin.
Discription of ye affection of ye mind.
Comp'n for English Justice of ye Peace.
Directions for leading a dev. Life.
The Temple—Sacred Poems.
Divine Poems.
Millans (?) Ann'l Register.
Riders English Miller.
Hist'y of ye Heathen Gods.
English Rougues & Others Extra.
Discourse of ye Uncertainty (?) Human Evidence.
Seven Wise Masters of R. (?).
Steel's Plays.
Old abridgm't Virg'a Laws.
Poems on Divine & m'l Subjects.
Dissertation on the Thebean Legion.
Boyle on ye Saltness of ye Sea.
Zingis a Tartarian Hist'y.
Defects in ye Reform't'n of ye Church of England.
Methods to Understand Roman H'y, by T. Brown
Vision of Purgatory
Misteries of Love and Eloq'ne.
Seven Champions of Chr'm.
Compleat Housewife.
Decay of Piety.
Ladys Travels.
Ramble (Rambler?).
Ropin's Reflect'n on Aristotle.
Radcliffe's Prescriptions.
Turkish Spy, 5th Vol.
Present for Ladies.
Thoughts in sad times.
The Sirpensary.
Hicks Devotions.
Plato's Works, 1st Vol.
Flower pieces—Miscel'y Poems.
Emblems Divine & moral.
Shakespeare's Works.

The Lover's Watch
Gazetteer.
Sherlock's Sermons.
Compleat Gamester.
Hoyles Games.
Memoir of Gamesters.
Tully's Offices.
Select Novels.
New System of Agriculture.
Discourse on ye 4 last things.
Memoirs of Savoy.
Reil's Anatomy.
Proposals to the Ladies.
Secret History of ye R. of King Charles & K'g James ye 2d.
State of London.
Norris's Poems &c.
Men & Women display'd.
English Orater.
Butler's Posthumous Works, 3 Vols.
Derham's Physico—Theology, 2 vols.
    Do. Astro Theology.
Prior on Tar Water.
Plague in London, 1665.
Voyages & Travels of Sir Jno: Mandeville.

(There were about 457 volumes in the collection, not including those which were missing when the list was made.)

*From: *The Virginia Magazine of History and Biography*, Vol. *XVII*,
December, 1909, pp. 404-412.

APPENDIX V

The Library of John Parke Custis, Esq., of
Fairfax County, Virginia

Transcribed in June 1927 by Charles Arthur Hoppin, from pages
274, 279, 280, 281, 282, 283, 284, 285 of "Will's etc. D., No. I, Fairfax
County."*

"Fairfax sst, Feby. Court 1782. Ordered that George Gilpin,
William Herbert, Charles Little & Thomas Herbert or any three of
them being first sworn according to Law inventory and appraise all
and Singular the Estate of John Parke Custis, Esqr. dec^d. in the
County of Fairfax which shall be Presented to their View and that the
Administrators return the Same to the next Court. P. Wagener"

The inventory was delivered into court by Lund Washington,

superintendent of Mount Vernon during the War of the American Revolution, on 18 September 1782. The appraisal of the personal property alone totaled £6559-5-6; in which inventory is the list of the books then remaining in the private library of the deceased intestate, viz:

	Ł.	S.	D.
"I Family Bible 20s/Vatelles Law of Nations 24/	2	4	0
Milton's works 2 volumes 30/Hatton's Mert. Magazine 2/	1	12	0
Hervey's Principles of Philosophy 2/6		2	6
Boerhaave's Method of Chymistry 12/Littleton's Dictionary 2 vols. 40/	2	12	0
Roman Antiquities, Robinson's Grecian & Roman Language	0	1	6
Dunsworth's Dictionary 30/Bentley's Phe edrus Fables 12/	2	3	0
Banks's Plays 2/6 Lee's Plays 2/6 D'Ursey's Plays 2/6	0	7	6
Campbell's Vitruvius 3 vols. 60/Virginia Laws 3 vols. 30/	4	10	0
Country Justice 6/English atlas 30/Walls's atlas 20/	2	16	0
Florilegis Magni 6/Senecas Philosophy 5/	0	11	0
Le Estrange's Asops fables 10/History of Queen Elizabeth 2/6	0	12	6
Guide to the practical physician	0	3	0
Fuller's History of the Wortheys of England	0	5	0
Cowley's works 6/Salmon's Botologir 12/	0	18	0
Wheverat's Travels 5/Brown's Travels 5/	0	10	0
Chamber's Dictionary 10/Sentimental Journal 3/	0	13	0
St. Muliezus Abridged 5/Cockburn on the Gonnoria 5/	0	10	0
Paxton on Disases 4/Fuller on Medicine 4/	0	8	0
Lubb on the Stone 6/Bannier on Medicine 3/	0	9	0
Keil on Anatomy 3/Bayle on Sea Water 1/	0	4	0
Shenston's works 2 vols. 6/Jones on fevers 2/6	0	8	6
Turner's Discourses 3/Wainwright on Naturals 3/	0	6	0
Cheyne on Health 4/Wiseman's Survery 5/	0	9	0
London Dispensatory 2/Springel;s Apharisms 4/	0	6	0
Cockburn on Fluxs 5/Pitt on physics 2/	0	7	0
Salmon's Dispensatory 2/Diver's Physicians Legacy 3/	0	5	0
Drake's system of Anatomy 2 vols. 8/Salmon's Physicians 2/	0	10	0
Baglivi's practical Physick 3/Strother on fevers 2/	0	5	0

Brown's Religes Medicine 1/Salmon's Dispensatory 2/	0	3	0
Salmon's Family Dictionary 2/Radcliff's Prescriptions 2 vols. 3/	0	5	0
Peachy on Diseases 6d. Physical & Chymical works 1/	0	1	6
Blair's Sermons 5 vols. 2/Duty of Man 5/	1	5	0
Chamberlayne on the Old Testament	0	2	0
Decay of Christian piety 4/Walton's Reflections 2/	0	6	0
South's Sermons 3/Goodman's Conference 2/6	0	5	6
Taylor's Holy living 4/Art of Contentments 2 vols. 4/	0	8	0
Lively Oracles 2/Barclay's Apology 6/	0	8	0
Animadversions on Congreve 5/Collier's Amendments. 1/	0	6	0
Welles's practice of Physick 2/White on fevers. 3/	0	5	0
Mandivel on Diseases 6/Doctors Scarrified 1/	0	7	0
Wiseman's Surgery 5/Salmon's Compent of Physk 2/	0	7	0
Sydenham's works 6/Jones on opium 3/	0	9	0
Turner on Diseases 4/Salmon's practice of physk. 2/	0	6	0
Quincey's Dispensatory 10/Clark's Salust 5/	0	15	0
Steels plays 1/Lucas's Memoirs 1/French Bible 2/	0	4	0
Ceasar's Commentarys and Ovids Tristivius	0	2	0
Garrison's English Exercises 3/English Justin 6d	0	3	6
Hudibras 5/Clarendon's History of the Rebellion 5 vols. 20/	1	5	0
Pheadrus Fables. Terence Advise to a son clerks Introduction Vigeras works, Clark's Erasmus Florius Socrates Orations, Accidents, Fretch's Acct. of Sicily & Ceasars Commentaries Robinson's Dictionary & Scarron's novels (the whole)	0	15	0
Ropin's Reflections 1/Milton's poms 1/Greek testament 1/	0	3	0
Brown's works 2 vols. 3/lecturs on religious subjects 1/	0	4	0
Clark Eutopia 2/Books 2/Brown's works 1/	0	5	0
Farquhars works 1/Guardian 2/Horace 2/	0	5	0
Walker's Lat. phrases 1/Greek Lexicon 20/ Milburn's notes 3/	1	4	0
Behn's Lovers Watch 1/Winterton's Homer 6/	0	7	0
Salmon's art of drawing 2/Dryden's Satires 4/	0	6	0
Cowley's Dictionary 2/Books 6/latin Dictionary 4/	0	12	0
Quintilian's work 2 do. 3/History of Erastus 1/	0	4	0
Collier's view of the English State 4/Poems on Divine Subjects 2/	0	6	0

Bales latin songs 6d/History of the prince of Bohemia 1/	0	1	6
Dissertation on the ban Legion 1/Review of Collier 4/	0	5	0
Creeche's Lucretia 2/6 Excise Bill 5/No Excise 4/	0	11	6
Collier's answer 2/6 Gentleman's calling 2/6 Waller's Poems 5/	0	10	0
Hait's poems 4/Miscellany poems 5/Dryden's Juvenal 6/	0	15	0
Fartasian History 6d/Greek Grammar 2/Hesiod 1/	0	9	0
Dryden's Miscellany poems 10/Bragtrill's Parthinia 6d/	0	10	6
Ferguson's History of Civil Society 6/Ovid's Travesty 2/	0	8	0
Revolution politicks 5/Political State 5 vols. 20/	1	5	0
Astry's charge to grand Jury 2/Government of the tongue 2/	0	4	0
Miscellany poems 2/Kings state of protestants in Ireland 3/	0	5	0
Disolation of France 2/Government of a wife 2/ Ovid's Epistles 3/	0	7	0
Turrence in English 4/Creeches Horace 3/	0	7	0
Gentlemen Instructed 5/Letters on wit & Politics 4/	0	9	0
History of England 2 vols. 5/Gullivers travels 2 vols. 8/	0	13	0
London Spy 4 vols. 16/Marshall's Epigrams 3/	0	19	0
Theory of the Earth 5/Gun-powder plot 1/	0	6	0
Miscellanious essays 3/Gibson's Farmery 4/Oldham's works 3/	0	10	0
Bacon's Essays 3/. the speculist 3/Craftsman 15 vols. 42/	2	8	0
Freeholder 3/Guardian 2 vols. 3/	0	6	0
Independent Whig 3 Vols. 9/Asburns Miscellanies 3/	0	12	0
Turkish Spy 9 vols. 27/Catoes Letters 4 vols. 12/	1	19	0
Tatler 4 vols. 12/Freethinker 3 vols. 9/Miscellany poems 3/	1	4	0
Duncan's Elements of Logick 3/Fordyce of Morals philosophy 3/	0	6	0
British Platarch 12 vols. 24/Hutcherson's Elements of Ethicks 4/	1	8	0
Collin's Ancient History 12 vols. 36/Cicero's Orations 20 vols. 60/	4	6	0
Rollin's Bills letters 3 vols. 18/Potter's antiquities of Greece 2 vols 12/	1	10	0

	£	s	d
Robertson's History of Scotland 2 vols.	0	12	0
Humes History of England 8 vols.	2	8	0
Guthrey's & Gray's history of the world 10 vols	3	0	0
McCauley's History of England 8 vols.	1	4	0
Proceedings of the house of Commons 4 vols.	1	4	0
Debates in the house of Commons 8 vols	2	8	0
Hook's Roman History 9 vols. 81/Salmons Grammar 8/	4	9	0
Packs lines 1/ 2 common prayer books 10/	0	11	0
Select Trials 2/Gay's Fables 2/State Trials 4/	0	8	0
No Excise Conelius Nepos 4/Creech's Lucretia 3/	0	7	0
Walker on English Particles 3/Gradus et parnasius 3/	0	6	0
Ovid's metomorpheses 5/Virgil 12/Horace 12/	1	9	0
Cicero's nations Lat; 4/Anderson 3/Greek testament 6/	0	13	0
Ovid 6/Latin bible 6/Juvenal 4/	0	16	0
Conjugal lewdness 3/Scalliger's Catullus 10/Salust 4/	0	17	0
Greek Lexicon 6/Greek Testament 6/Greek Grammar 3/	0	15	0
Quintius Curtius 8/latin prayer book 2/Living 4 vols. 16/	1	6	0
Patrick's Homer 5/Marshal Epigrams 8/Gilbeas 4/	0	17	0
Latin psalms 3/Greek Rudiments 3/Ceasar's Commentaries 1/6	0	7	6
Stone's Euclid 7/6 Mair's bookkeeping 6/	0	13	6
Lock on understanding 2 vols. 12/Burlemague on nat. pol. law 12/	1	4	0
Religious poems 6/King's origin of Evil 7/6	0	13	6
Gerard's Dissertations 6/Art of Speaking 5/Walls Logick 6/	0	17	0
Brown's Essays 5/Kennett's Roman Antiquities 6/	0	11	0
Puffendorff's Law of nature & Nations 6/	0	6	0
Wallaston's Religion of nature 6/Beattie on truth 6/	0	12	0
Read's Inquiry 5/Kennett's Roman Antiquities 6/	0	11	0
Turnbull's principles of moral philosophy 2 vols.	0	12	0
Sharp in defence of Christianity 2 vols.	0	6	0
Sharp's introduction to History 5/Smith's moral sentiments 5/	0	10	0
Martin's philosophical Grammar	0	6	0
Dignity of human nature 2 vols.	0	10	0
Turnbull's system of universal law 2 vols	0	10	0
Conybear's Defense of revealed Religion	0	4	0
Lock of Government	0	5	0

Bushworth's Institutes of natural law 2 vols.	0	12	0
Montesque's spirit of law 12/Grotious 2 vols. 12/	1	4	0
Blackwall's sacred classicks 2 vols. 6/Clark's Grotious 2/.	0	8	0
Squires on natural & Revealed religion	2	0	0
Matho 2 vols. 6/Thompson's works 4 vols. 12	0	16	0
Voltaire's works 36 vols 108/Pope's works 4 vols 12/	6	0	0
Swift's works 4 vols. 12/Spectator 5 vols 15/	1	7	0
Horace 3/Blackerley's Justice of Peace 2/	0	5	0
24 vols by different authors	0	12	0
Durham's sermons 2/6 Ditto Survey of the heavens 2/6	0	5	0
Norris's poems 2/Entinks spelling dictionary 4/	0	6	0
Pocket Atlas 3/Storke's Justice of peace 10/	0	13	0
Journey thro China 6/Voyage to the levant 4/	0	10	0
Dampries Voyages 4 vols. 24/Resolutions of Sweden 4	1	8	0
The Ladyes calling 2/6 Robinson Crusoe 2 vols. 6/	0	8	6
Arrivals of King George 2,5/Echards Roman History 2 vols 10/	0	15	0
Willwoods memoirs 5/Osburnes miscellany 2/6	0	7	6
Abridgment of Sir Walter Raleigh 3/Duke's (?) history of England and Scotland 5/	0	8	0
Holly memoirs 3/Behns poems 3/	0	6	0
Plutarchs lives 5 vols. 20/Ratcliff poems 1/	1	1	0
Life of Oliver Cromwell 5/Knoxes voyages 42/	2	7	0
Compleat Tradesman 2 vols 6/Wingates arthmetick 2/	0	8	0
Pools parnassus 2/Echards Gazeteer 4/	0	6	0
Panegyrick on Tragen 2/Human judgement 2/6	0	4	6
Abridgment of plots 2/6 Steven's songs 2/	0	4	6
Lives of Ceasars 3/Miltons defense 2/6	0	5	6
Secret History of Charles 2nd and James 2nd	0	2	0
State of England 2/6 Rochesters letters 2/6	0	5	0
Dudleys poems 6 vols 26/Fishers companion 4/	1	10	0
Select novels 2/Lock on Education 3/	0	5	0
Fishers Arithmetick 3/Plutarchs morals 5 vols. 20/	1	3	0
Milton's paradise 6/Brochens Farmery 6/	0	12	0
Natural History of Florida vols. in folio	15		0
Don Quixote 4 vols 12/Compleat Housewife 3/	0	15	0

*From: *Tyler's Quarterly Historical and Geneological Magazine*, Vol. IX, 1928, pp. 97-103.

APPENDIX VI

Inventory of books at Mount Vernon — Lund Washington
July 23, 1783

Gibsons Diseases of Horses
The Compleat Horseman or Perfect Farrier by Sir Wm. Hope
The Sportsman Dictionary or Country Gentlemen Companion
Longley on Gardening
Millers Gardeners Dictionary
Quimsey Dispensitory
Advice to the people in general by Doctr. Tissott
Virginia Laws or Acts of Assembly
    Do   Do   by John Mercer
Justice of the Peace in 4 Vol: by Richd. Burn
The Attorneys Pocket Book 2 Vol:
Smollets History of England 9 Vols:
Annual Register for 1750, 1759, 1760 & 1761
Museum Rusticum 6 Vol:
A Compleat Body of Husbandry by Thos. Hob (sic) 4 Vol:
Handmaid to the Arts. 2 Vol:
Maxwells practicle Husbandry
Observation on Husbandry by Edward Lyle—2 Vol:
Farmers Compleat Guide
A new sistem of Agriculture or a speedy method of Growg. Rich
Female Fortune Hunters in 3 Vol:
Telemachus—2 Vol:
Lord Lansdown 3 Vol:
Tom Jones 4 Vol:
Tour through Great Briton 4 Vol:
Bossus (sic) Travel through Louisiana—2Vol:
Memorials of the Noted Horse 2 Vol:
David Ranger 2 Vol:
Miltons Poems 2 Vol:
Pope's Works 1st. 2d. & 5th Vol:
Perigrine Pickle
Guardian / 2 Vol:
Spectators
History of Virginia
History of Algiers
Geographical Grammer
A Compleat View of the British Customs
Young's Night Thoughts
Female Fables
Life of Mahomad
Gazetteers

Bailey's Dictionary
Voyage Round the World Lord Ancon
Senaca's Morrals
English Grammar
Cyrus's Travels
Soloman & Alabama
Compleat Gamester by Seymore
Hoile's Games
Inocent imposture or Supposed Daughters
Nature Displayed by Wm. Humphreys
The Life of Oliver Cromwell
Yorrichs Sermons—2 Vol:
The Wisdom of God in the Creation
Sick Men Visited
Churchill's Sermons
Exposition of the 39 Articles of the Church of England
Trial of the 7 Bishops
Dissertation on the Mosaical Creation
Several Old Sermon and Religious Books that probably will never be
    read again—I did not think worth listing
Some pamphlets, plays, &c. &c. of but little worth
Henry Daggs Esqr. on Criminal Law 3 Vol: unbound

The above are a List of Books now at Mount Vernon

A List of Books at Mt. Vern.
    23d. July 1783

(This note is in the handwriting of General Washington. The list was
    made by Lund, quoting Dr. J. C. Fitzpatrick)

1783 Aug. 13 Newburg G/W to Lund Washington: I have received
    your Letter of the 30th Ult°. with a Catalogue of my Books—
    When you go next to Abingdon, see if there is any there with my
    name or Arms in them, & for^{d} the list.

FOOTNOTES
Chapter I

1. William Stearns Davis, **Life in Elizabethan days, a picture of a typical English community at the end of the sixteenth century.** (New York: Harper & Row, 1930), p. 140.

2. C. Waller Barrett, "The American literary background of George Washington's time" (address to the annual meeting of the Mount Vernon Ladies' Association, October 23, 1965), p. 2 (Mimeographed).

3. Hamilton Wright Mabie, **American ideals, character and life** (New York: Macmillan, 1913), p. 94.

4. Barrett, p. 1.

5. Charles M. Andrews, **Pilgrims and Puritans, Part II: Colonial folkways** (New Haven: Yale University Press, 1919), p. 152.

6. Elise Lathrop, **Historic houses of early America** (New York: Tudor Publishing Company, 1935), p. 31.

7. Gordon Carruth, **The encyclopedia of American facts and dates** (4th ed., New York: Thomas Y. Crowell, 1966), p. 14.

8. Louis B. Wright, **The cultural life of the American colonies, 1607-1763** (New York: Harper & Brothers, 1957), p. 144.

9. Edwin Tunis, **Colonial craftsmen and the beginnings of American industry** (Cleveland: World Publishing Company, 1965), p. 126.

10. Andrews, Part II, p. 152.

11. Wright, p. 136.

12. Jackson Turner Main, **The social structure of Revolutionary America** (Princeton: Princeton University Press, 1965), pp. 254-260; Andrews, p. 152.

13. Carruth, p. 8.

14. Daniel J. Boorstin, **The landmark history of the American people from Plymouth to Appomattox** (New York: Random House, 1968), p. 123.

15. Dixon Ryan Fox, **Ideas in motion,** Appleton-Century Historical Essays (New York: Appleton-Century, 1935), p. 26.

16. Edward Humphrey, ed., **The American people's encyclopedia, a modern reference work** (New York: Grolier Incorporated, 1962), p. 73; Boorstin, p. 42.

17. Daniel J. Boorstin, **The Americans, the colonial experience** (New York: Random House, 1958), p. 303.

18. Louis B. Wright, **The Atlantic frontier, colonial American civilization, 1607-1763** (Ithaca, New York: Cornell University Press, 1965), p. 153.

19. Carruth, p. 32.

20. Boorstin, The Americans, the colonial experience, p. 302.

21. Wright, The cultural life of the American colonies, p. 144.

22. G. M. Trevelyan, Illustrated English social history, Vol. 3: The eighteenth century (New York: David McKay, 1965), p. 117.

23. Boorstin, The Americans, the colonial experience, p. 302.

24. John D. Hicks, The federal union, a history of the United States to 1865 (2nd ed., Boston: Houghton Mifflin Company, 1948), p. 75.

25. Charles A. Beard and Mary R. Beard, The rise of American civilization (New York: Macmillan, 1937), p. 145.

26. Sydney George Fisher, Men, women and manners in Colonial times, Vol. I (Philadelphia: J. B. Lippincott, 1898), p. 109.

27. Boorstin, The Americans, the colonial experience, p. 302.

28. John T. Faris, Real stories from our history, romance and adventure in authentic records of the development of the United States (Boston: Ginn and Company, 1916), p. 67.

29. Margaret Cousins, Ben Franklin in Old Philadelphia (New York: Random House, 1952), p. 80.

30. Faris, pp. 66-70.

31. Merle Curti, The growth of American thought (2nd ed., New York: Harper and Brothers, 1943), pp. 42-43.

32. Letter from the Redwood Library.

33. Harvey Wish, Society and thought in early America, Vol. I (New York: Longmans, Green, 1953), p. 61.

34. Curti, p. 42.

35. Richard Bissell, You can always tell a Harvard man (New York: McGraw-Hill Book Company, 1962), pp. 24-25 and 158-159.

36. Fox, p. 13.

37. Curti, p. 82.

38. Andrews, Part II, p. 157.

39. Fiske Kimball, American architecture (New York: Bobbs-Merrill, 1928), p. 71.

40. Library of Congress, A guide to the study of the United States of America, representative books reflecting the development of American life and thought (Washington, D.C.: Reference Department, Library of Congress, 1960), p. 1071.

41. Ishbel Ross, **Taste in America, an illustrated history of the evolution of architecture, furnishings, fashions, and customs of the American people** (New York: Thomas Y. Crowell, 1967), p. 31.

42. Boorstin, **The Americans, the colonial experience,** p. 303.

43. Marcus Cunliffe, **George Washington, man and monument** (Boston: Little, Brown and Co., 1958), p. 29.

44. W. E. Woodward, **George Washington, the image and the man** (New York: Blue Ribbon Books, 1926), p. 115.

45. Barrett, p. 2.

46. Benson J. Lossing, **The home of Washington, or Mount Vernon and its associations, historical, biographical and pictorial** (Hartford, Conn.: A. S. Hale, 1870), pp. 37-38.

47. Cunliffe, pp. 30-31.

48. Samuel Eliot Morison, "The young man Washington" in **George Washington, a profile,** ed. by James Morton Smith (New York: Hill and Wang, 1969), p. 42.

49. Thomas G. Fleming, **Affectionately yours, George Washington; a self-portrait in letters of friendship** (New York: W. W. Norton and Company, 1967), p. 12.

50. Cunliffe, p. 31.

51. Cunliffe, p. 32.

52. Sol Bloom, "Questions and answers pertaining to the life and time of George Washington" in **History of the George Washington Bicentennial Celebration,** Vol. III: **Literature Series** (Washington, D.C.: United States George Washington Bicentennial Commission, 1932), p. 654.

53. Woodward, p. 28.

54. Albert Bushnell Hart, "Washington, the man of mind" Part I, "Practical Education" in **History of the George Washington Bicentennial Celebration,** Vol. I: **Literature Series** (Washington, D.C.: United States George Washington Bicentennial Commission, 1932), p. 18.

55. Lossing, p. 79.

56. Woodward, p. 74.

57. Morison, pp. 46-48.

58. Cunliffe, p. 59.

59. Walton C. John and Alma H. Preinkert, "The educational views of George Washington, based on his letters, diaries, and addresses" Chapter I, "His early education" in **History of the George Washington Bicentennial Celebration,** Vol. I: **Literature Series** (Washington, D.C.: United States George Washington Bicentennial Commission, 1932), p. 527; Woodward, p. 25.

Chapter II

1. Gerald W. Johnson, **Mount Vernon: The story of a shrine.** . . (New York: Random House, 1953), p. 58.

2. Charles C. Wall, "Notes on the early history of Mount Vernon," **The William and Mary Quarterly,** II, No. 2, Third Series (April, 1945), p. 190.

3. Benson J. Lossing, **The home of Washington; or Mount Vernon and its associations, historical, biographical, and pictorial** (Hartford, Conn.: A. S. Hale, 1870), p. 54.

4. Warren D. Brush, "The building of Mount Vernon Mansion," **House Beautiful,** LI, No. 2 February, 1922, pp. 163-4.

5. Wallace Nutting, **Virginia beautiful** (Garden City, New York: Garden City Publishing Company, Inc., 1935), p. 188.

6. Thomas E. Tallmadge, **The story of architecture in America** (New York: W. W. Norton & Company, Inc., 1936), p. 44.

7. Brush, p. 163.

8. Edith Tunis Sale, **Colonial interiors, Southern Colonial and early Federal** (New York: Bonanza Books, 1930), p. 2.

9. Paul Wilstach, **Tidewater Maryland** (Indianapolis: Bobbs-Merrill Company, 1931), p. 327.

10. Fiske Kimball, **Domestic architecture of the American colonies and of the early Republic** (New York: Charles Scribner's Sons, 1922), p. 56.

11. Harold Donaldson Eberlein, **The architecture of Colonial America** (Boston: Little, Brown, and Company, 1915), p. 121.

12. Talbot Hamlin, **Benjamin Henry Latrobe** (New York: Oxford University Press, 1955), pp. 75-76.

13. Martin S. Briggs, **Goths and Vandals, a study of the destruction, neglect, and preservation of historical buildings in England** (London: Constable Publishers, 1952), p. 124.

14. Lossing, pp. 108-114.

15. The Mount Vernon Ladies' Association of the Union, Mount Vernon (Mount Vernon, Virginia: the Association, 1974), p. 71.

16. Paul Wilstach, **Mount Vernon, Washington's home and the nation's shrine** (Garden City, New York: Doubleday, Page & Company, 1916), p. 78.

17. Wilstach, Mount Vernon, p. 196.

18. Johnson, p. 60.

19. Elswyth Thane, **Mount Vernon, the legacy** (Philadelphia & New York: J. B. Lippincott Company, 1967), p. 96.

20. Brush, p. 164.

21. John Gloag, **Guide to Western architecture** (London: George Allen and Unwin, Ltd., 1958), p. 250.

22. Lossing, p. 226.

23. Thane, p. 132.

24. Kimball, p. 50.

25. William Barrow Floyd, "The portraits and paintings at Mount Vernon, 1754-1799, Part I," **Antiques,** C, No. 5 (November, 1971), p. 770.

26. George Washington Parke Custis, **Recollections and private memoirs of Washington** . . . (Philadelphia: J. W. Bradley, 1859), p. 156.

27. Morley Jeffers Williams, "Washington's changes at Mount Vernon plantation," **Landscape Architecture,** XXVIII, No. 2 (January, 1938), 69.

28. Marshall B. Davidson, **The American Heritage history of notable American houses** (New York: American Heritage Publishing Co. Inc., 1971), p. 12.

29. Ettore Camesasca, ed., **History of the house** (New York: G. P. Putnam's Sons, 1971), p. 374.

30. Davidson, p. 97.

31. Brush, p. 163.

32. Davidson, p. 97.

33. R. T. H. Halsey and Elizabeth Tower, **The homes of our ancestors as shown in the American Wing of the Metropolitan Museum of Art of New York** (Garden City, Long Island: Doubleday, Doran and Company, Inc. at the Country Life Press, 1925), p. 117.

Chapter III

1. R. T. H. Halsey and Elizabeth Tower, **The homes of our ancestors as shown in the American Wing of the Metropolitan Museum of Art of New York** (Garden City, Long Island: Doubleday, Doran and Company, Inc. at the Country Life Press, 1925), p. 119.

2. Helen Comstock, **100 most beautiful rooms in America** (New York: Bonanza Books, 1965), p. 138.

3. Helen Maggs Fede, **Washington furniture at Mount Vernon** (Mount Vernon, Virginia: The Mount Vernon Ladies' Association of the Union, 1966), p. 17.

4. Benson J. Lossing, **The home of Washington; or Mount Vernon and its associations, historical, biographical, and pictorial** (Hardford, Conn.: A. S. Hale, 1870), p. 252.

5. Halsey, p. 116.

6. Halsey, p. 106.

7. Paul H. Burroughs, **Southern antiques** (New York: Bonanza Books, 1967), p. 77.

8. Thomas Hamilton Ormsbee, **The story of American furniture** (New York: Macmillan Company, 1934), p. 93.

9. Halsey, p. 112.

10. Ettore Camesasca, ed., **History of the house** (New York: G. P. Putnam's Sons, 1971), p. 424.

11. Halsey, pp. 152-153.

12. Edwin Valentine Mitchell, **American village** (New York: Stackpole Sons, 1938), pp. 201-202.

13. Burroughs, p. 10.

14. Burroughs, p. 128.

15. **Annual Report, The Mount Vernon Ladies' Association of the Union, 1948,** p. 25.

16. Lossing, pp. 175-177.

17. **Annual Report, The Mount Vernon Ladies' Association of the Union, 1967,** pp. 12-13.

18. **Annual Report, 1948,** p. 25.

19. **Annual Report, 1967,** pp. 11-12.

20. Winslow C. Watson, ed., **Men & times of the Revolution or memoirs of Elkanah Watson** (New York: Dana & Co., 1857), p. 137.

21. Lossing, p. 50.

22. Mansion Library Notebook, unpaged.

23. Mansion Library Notebook, unpaged.

24. Lossing, p. 80.

25. Mansion Library Notebook, unpaged.

26. Charles Nagel, **American furniture, 1650-1850, a brief background and illustrated history** (New York: Chanticleer Press, 1949), p. 66.

27. Davidson, p. 153.

Chapter IV

1. Gene Gurney and Clare Gurney, **Mount Vernon** (New York: Franklin Watts, 1965), p. 23; **Morgan Beatty's your nation's capitol,** (New York: Farrar, Straus and Cudahy, 1956), p. 171.

2. James Hosmer Penniman, "Washington proprietor of Mount Vernon" Part I, "The estate" in **History of the George Washington Bicentennial Celebration,** Vol. I: **Literature Series** (Washington, D.C.: George Washington Bicentennial Commission, 1932), p. 97.

3. "George Washington the leader of men" in **History of the George Washington Bicentennial Celebration,** Vol. I: **Literature Series** (Washington, D.C.: George Washington Bicentennial Commission, 1932), p. 264.

4. Penniman, p. 97.

5. "George Washington the leader of men," p. 264.

6. John C. Fitzpatrick, "Washington as a religious man" Part I, "George Washington and religion" in **History of the George Washington Bicentennial Celebration** (Washington, D.C.: George Washington Bicentennial Commission, 1932), p. 50.

7. Schroeder-Lossing, **Life and times of Washington** (Albany, New York: M. M. Belcher Publishing Company, 1903), p. 29.

8. Schroeder-Lossing, p. 19; "The mother of George Washington" in **History of the George Washington Bicentennial Celebration,** Vol. I: **Literature Series** (Washington, D.C.: George Washington Bicentennial Commission, 1932), p. 232.

9. Benson J. Lossing, **The home of Washington, or Mount Vernon and its associations, historical, biographical and pictorial** (Hartford, Conn.: A. S. Hale, 1870), p. 33.

10. Samuel Eliot Morison, "The young man Washington" in **George Washington, a profile,** ed. by James Morton Smith (New York: Hill and Wang, 1969), p. 45.

11. Lossing, p. 57.

12. Lossing, p. 393.

13. "George Washington, the leader of men," p. 264.

14. Dixon Wecter, "President Washington and Parson Weems" in **George Washington, a profile,** ed. by James Morton Smith (New York: Hill and Wang, 1969), p. 3.

15. Gerald W. Johnson, **Mount Vernon, the story of a shrine** (New York: Random House, 1953), p. 74.

16. Marvin Kitman, **George Washington's expense account** (New York: Simon and Schuster, 1970), p. 22.

17. Elswyth Thane, **Mount Vernon, the legacy** (New York: Lippincott, 1967), p. 222.

18. David M. Matteson, "Washington the farmer" Part III, "Washington's scientific farm methods" in **History of the George Washington Bicentennial Celebration** (Washington, D.C.: George Washington Bicentennial Commission, 1932), p. 45.

19. Correspondence in the files of the Mount Vernon Ladies' Association of the Union.

20. Eugene E. Prussing, **The estate of George Washington, deceased** (Boston: Little, Brown, and Company, 1927), p. 429.

21. Marcus Cunliffe, **George Washington, man and monument** (Boston: Little, Brown, and Company, 1958), p. 62.

22. William J. Johnson, **George Washington, the Christian** (New York: Abingdon Press, 1919), p. 48.

23. Elswyth Thane, **Mount Vernon family** (New York: Crowell-Collier Press, 1968), pp. 18-20, p. 71.

24. Bernhard Knollenberg, **George Washington, the Virginia period, 1732-1775** (Durham, North Carolina: Duke University Press, 1964), pp. 73-74.

25. Knollenberg, p. 74.

26. "Catalogue of the library of Daniel Parke Custis," **Virginia Magazine of History and Biography,** XVII (October-December, 1909), 404-12.

27. C. Waller Barrett, "The American literary background of George Washington's time" (address to the annual meeting of the Mount Vernon Ladies' Association, October 23, 1965), pp. 9-10. (Mimeographed).

28. William H. Wilbur, **The making of George Washington** (Deland, Florida: Patriotic Education, 1970), p. 176.

29. Paul Wilstach, **Mount Vernon, Washington's home and the nation's shrine** (Garden City, New York: Doubleday, Page & Company, 1916), p. 115.

30. Wilstach, p. 124.

31. Lossing, p. 107.

32. Lossing, p. 79.

33. James Thomas Flexner, "Cincinnatus assayed: Washington in the Revolution" in **George Washington, a profile,** ed. by James Morton Smith (New York: Hill and Wang, 1969), p. 93.

34. Wilstach, p. 137.

35. Johnson, p. 85.

36. Kitman, p. 22.

37. Lossing, p. 123.

38. Barrett, p. 10.

39. "The library of John Parke Custis, esq., of Fairfax County, Virginia," **Tyler's Quarterly Historical and Genealogical Magazine,** IX (1928), 97-103.

40. Harriet C. Towner, The Mount Vernon library (Mount Vernon, Virginia: Mount Vernon Ladies' Association of the Union, 1937), p. 12.

41. Wilstach, p. 157.

42. Wilstach, p. 164; Thane, Mount Vernon, the legacy, p. 222.

43. Cunliffe, p. 130.

44. Jared Sparks, The life of Washington (New York: A. T. Burt Company, 1902), pp. 371-372.

45. Penniman, p. 97.

46. Wilstach, pp. 178-180.

47. Lossing, pp. 206-207.

48. Samuel Eliot White, "George Washington as an administrator" in George Washington, a profile, ed. by James Morton Smith (New York: Hill and Wang, 1969), p. 227.

49. Barrett, p. 11.

50. Wilstach, p. 190.

51. John T. Faris, Real stories from our history: romance and adventure in authentic records of the development of the United States (Boston: Ginn and Company, 1916), pp. 68 and 70.

52. Towner, p. 11.

53. Lossing, p. 290.

54. Thane, Mount Vernon family, p. 79.

55. Edwin Tunis, Colonial craftsmen and the beginnings of American industry (Cleveland: World Publishing Company, 1965), pp. 98-100.

56. Letters and recollections of George Washington, being letters to Tobias Lear and others between 1790 and 1799, showing the First American in the management of his estate and domestic affairs (New York: Doubleday, Page & Company, 1906), p. 176.

57. Thane, Mount Vernon, the legacy, p. 196.

58. Penniman, p. 97.

59. Towner, p. 8.

60. Daniel J. Boorstin, The Americans, the colonial experience (New York: Random House, 1958), p. 303.

61. Appleton P. C. Griffin, comp., A catalogue of the Washington collection in the Boston Atheneum (Cambridge, Mass.: University Press, 1897), p. 481.

62. Prussing, p. 201.

63. Gurney, p. 24; Prussing, p. 139.

64. Towner, p. 6; Wyman W. Parker, "Henry Stevens sweeps the states," **Papers of the Bibliographical Society of America,** 52 (Fourth Quarter, 1958), 255.

65. Towner, p. 6; Parker, p. 255.

66. Parker, pp. 249-61.

67. Towner, p. 6.

68. Prussing, p. 141.

69. Mansion Library Notebook, unpaged.

70. Towner, p. 6.

71. "George Washington the man of action in military and civil life" in **History of the George Washington Bicentennial Celebration,** Vol. 1: **Literature Series** (Washington, D.C.: George Washington Bicentennial Commission, 1932), p. 249.

72. Towner, p. 6.

73. Van Allen Bradley, "Book Collecting," **World Book Encyclopedia,** 1976 edition, II, 380.

74. John Carter, "The private library in America," **American Libraries,** 4, No. 11 (December, 1973), 665-7.

75. Walton C. John, "The educational views of George Washington, based on his letters, diaries and addresses," in **History of the George Washington Bicentennial Celebration** (Washington, D.C.: George Washington Bicentennial Commission, 1932), p. 536.

76. J. Winston Coleman, ed., **Kentucky, a pictorial history** (Lexington: University Press of Kentucky, 1971), p. 139.

77. Prussing, p. 28.

78. "George Washington, the leader of men," p. 262; Prussing, p. 28.

79. Prussing, p. 29.

SELECTED BIBLIOGRAPHY

Adams, James Truslow, ed. **Dictionary of American history.** New York: Scribner's, 1940.

American Heritage book of great historic places. New York: Simon & Schuster, 1957.

Andrews, Charles M. **Pilgrims and puritans.** Part I: **The fathers of New England.** Part II: **Colonial folkways.** New Haven: Yale University Press, 1919.

Andrews, Marietta Minnigerode. **George Washington's country.** New York: E. P. Dutton and Company, 1930.

Aronson, Joseph. **The encyclopedia of furniture.** 3rd ed. New York: Crown Publishers, 1965.

Barrett, C. Waller. "**The American literary background of George Washington's time.**" Address at the annual meeting of the Mount Vernon Ladies' Association of the Union, October 23, 1965.

Beatty, Morgan. **Your nation's capitol.** New York: Farrar, Straus and Cudahy, 1956.

Beard, Charles A., and Beard, Mary R. **The rise of American civilization.** New York: Macmillan, 1937.

Bissell, Richard. **You can always tell a Harvard man.** New York: McGraw-Hill Book Company, 1962.

Blake, Peter. **The master builders.** New York: Knopf, 1960.

Boller, Paul F. **George Washington and religion.** Dallas, Texas: Southern Methodist University Press, 1963.

Boorstin, Daniel J. **The Americans, the colonial experience.** New York: Random House, 1958.

Boorstin, Daniel J. **The landmark history of the American people from Plymouth to Appomattox.** New York: Random House, 1968.

Borden, Morton, ed. **George Washington.** Englewood Cliffs, New Jersey: Prentice-Hall, 1969.

Bradley, Van Allen. "Book collecting." **World Book Encyclopedia,** 1976 ed. Vol. II.

Briggs, Martin S. **Goths and vandals, a study of the destruction, neglect, and preservation of historical buildings in England.** London: Constable Publishers, 1952.

Brush, Warren C. "The building of Mount Vernon Mansion." **House Beautiful,** LI, No. 2 ,February, 1922, 130-1 and 162-4.

Burroughs, Paul H. **Southern antiques.** New York: Bonanza Books, 1967.

Camesasca, Ettore, ed. History of the house. New York: G. P. Putnam's Sons, 1971.

Carruth, Gordon, ed. The encyclopedia of American facts and dates. 4th ed. New York: Thomas Y. Crowell, 1966.

"Catalogue of the library of Daniel Parke Custis." Virginia Magazine of History and Biography, XVII (December, 1909), 404-12.

Chambers, William. A treatise on the decorative part of civil engineering. New York: Benjamin Bloom, Inc., 1968.

Coleman, Oliver. Successful houses. New York: Fox Duffield & Company, 1906.

Comstock, Helen. 100 most beautiful rooms in America. New York: Bonanza Books, 1965.

Concise dictionary of American history. New York: Scribner's, 1962.

Cousins, Frank, and Riley, Phil M. The colonial architecture of Philadelphia. Boston: Little, Brown, and Company, 1920.

Cunliffe, Marcus. George Washington, man and monument. Boston: Little, Brown, and Company, 1958.

Curti, Merle. The growth of American thought. 2nd ed. New York: Harper and Brothers, 1943.

Custis, George Washington Parke. Recollections and private memoirs of Washington. Philadelphia: J. W. Bradley, 1861.

Davidson, Marshall B. The American Heritage history of notable American houses. New York: American Heritage Publishing Company, 1971.

Davis, William Stearns. Life in Elizabethan days, a picture of a typical English community at the end of the sixteenth century. New York: Harper & Row, 1930.

Dow, Joy Wheeler. American renaissance. New York: William T. Comstock, 1904.

Drury, John. The heritage of early American houses. New York: Coward-McCann, Inc., 1969.

Eberlein, Harold Donaldson. The architecture of colonial America. Boston: Little, Brown, and Company, 1915.

Faithfull, Emily. Three visits to America. New York: Fowler & Wells Company, 1884.

Faris, John T. Real stories from our history: romance and adventure in authentic records of the development of the United States. Boston: Ginn and Company, 1916.

Fede, Helen Maggs. Washington furniture at Mount Vernon. Mount Vernon, Virginia: The Mount Vernon Ladies' Association of the Union, 1966.

Fisher, Sydney George. **Men, women and manners in colonial times,** Vol. I. Philadelphia: J. B. Lippincott, 1898.

Fleming, Thomas J., ed. **Affectionately yours, George Washington; a self-portrait in letters of friendship.** New York: W. W. Norton, 1967.

Flexner, James Thomas. **George Washington, anguish and farewell** [1793-1799]. Boston: Little, Brown, and Company, 1964.

Flexner, James Thomas. **George Washington in the American Revolution** [1775-1783]. Boston: Little, Brown, and Company, 1967.

Floyd, William Barrow. "The portraits and paintings at Mount Vernon, 1754-1799, Part I." **Antiques,** C, No. 5 November, 1971, pp. 768-74.

Fox, Dixon Ryan. **Ideas in motion.** New York: D. Appleton-Century Company, 1935.

Gloag, John. **Guide to Western architecture.** London: George Allen and Unwin, 1958.

Glubock, Shirley, ed. **Home and child life in colonial days.** New York: Macmillan and Company, 1969.

Gowans, Alan. **Images of American living.** Philadelphia: J. B. Lippincott, 1964.

Grandjean, Etienne. **Ergonomics of the home.** New York: John Wiley, 1973.

Griffin, Appleton P.C., comp. **A catalogue of the Washington collection in the Boston Atheneum.** Cambridge, Mass.: University Press, 1897.

Gurney, Gene, and Gurney, Clare. **Mount Vernon.** New York: Franklin Watts, 1965.

Haas, Irvin. **America's historic houses and restorations.** New York: Castle Books, 1966.

Halsey, R.T.H., and Tower, Elizabeth. **The homes of our ancestors, as shown in the American Wing of the Metropolitan Museum of Art of New York.** Garden City, Long Island, N.Y.: Doubleday, Doran and Company, Inc. at the Country Life Press, 1925.

Hamlin, Talbot Faulkner. **The American spirit in architecture.** Vol. 13 of **The pageant of America.** New Haven, Conn.: Yale University Press, 1926.

Hamlin, Talbot Faulkner. **Architecture through the ages.** New York: G. P. Putnam's Sons, 1953.

Hamlin, Talbot Faulkner. **Benjamin Henry Latrobe.** New York: Oxford University Press, 1955.

Hicks, John D. **The federal union, a history of the United States to 1865.** 2nd ed. Boston: Houghton Mifflin Company, 1948.

Hornung, Clarence P. **Treasury of American design,** Vol. 2, New York: Harry N. Abrams.

Johnson, Gerald W. **Mount Vernon, the story of a shrine.** New York: Random House, 1953.

Johnson, Thomas H. **The Oxford companion to American history.** New York: Oxford University Press, 1966.

Johnson, William J. **George Washington the Christian.** New York: Abingdon Press, 1919.

Jones, Howard Mumford. **American and French culture.** Chapel Hill, North Carolina: University of North Carolina Press, 1927.

Jordan, R.F. **A concise history of Western architecture.** New York: Harcourt, Brace & World, Inc., 1970.

Kimball, Fiske. **American architecture.** New York: Bobbs-Merrill, 1928.

Kimball, Fiske. **Domestic architecture of the American colonies and of the early Republic.** New York: Charles Scribner's Sons, 1922.

King, David. **An historical sketch of the Redwood Library and Atheneum in Newport, Rhode Island.** Boston: John Wilson and Son, 1860.

Kitman, Marvin. **George Washington's expense account.** New York: Simon & Schuster, 1970.

Knollenberg, Bernhard. **George Washington, the Virginia period, 1732-1775.** Durham, North Carolina: Duke University Press. 1964.

Langdon, William Chauncey. **Everyday things in American life, 1776-1876.** New York: Scribner's, 1955.

Lathrop, Elise. **Historic houses of early America.** New York: Tudor Publishing Company, 1935.

Lees-Milne, James. **The age of Adam.** New York: B. t. Botsford, 1947.

Letters and recollections of George Washington, being letters to Tobias Lear and other between 1790 and 1799, showing the First American in the management of his estate and domestic affairs. New York: Doubleday, Page & Company, 1906.

Levin, Phyllis Lee. **Great historic houses of America.** New York: Coward-McCann, 1970.

Library of Congress Reference Department. **A guide to the study of the United States of America, representative books reflecting the development of American life and thought.** Washington, D.C.: Library of Congress, 1960.

"The library of John Parke Custis, esq., of Fairfax County, Virginia." **Tyler's Quarterly Historical and Geneological Magazine,** IX (1928), 97-103.

Lossing, Benson J. **The home of Washington, or Mount Vernon and its associations, historical, biographical, and pictorial.** Hartford, Conn.: A. S. Hale, 1870.

Mabie, Hamilton Wright. **American ideals, character and life.** New York: Macmillan Company, 1913.

Main, Jackson Turner. **The social structure of Revolutionary America.** Princeton, New Jersey: Princeton University Press. 1965.

Mitchell, Edwin Valentine. **American village.** New York: Stackpole Sons, 1938.

Morison, Samuel Eliot; Commager, Henry Steele; and Leuchtenburg, William E. **The growth of the American republic.** New York: Oxford University Press, 1969.

Morris, Richard B. **Encyclopedia of American history.** New York: Harper & Brothers, 1953.

Morris, Richard B. **The "Life" history of the United States.** Vol. I: **Prehistory to 1774, the New World.** New York: Time, Inc., 1963.

Morse, Frances Clary. **Furniture of the olden time.** New York: Macmillan Company, 1937.

Mount Vernon Ladies' Association of the Union. **Mount Vernon.** Mount Vernon, Virginia: The Association, 1974.

Nagel, Charles. **American furniture, 1650-1850.** New York: Chanticleer Press, 1949.

Northend, Mary H. **Colonial homes and their furnishings.** Boston: Little, Brown and Company, 1920.

Nutting, Wallace. **Virginia beautiful.** Garden City, New York: Garden City Publishing Company, Inc., 1935.

Ormsbee, Thomas Hamilton. **The story of American furniture.** New York: Macmillan Company, 1934.

Page, Thomas Nelson. **Mount Vernon and its preservation, 1858-1910.** New York: Knickerbocker Press, 1910.

Parker, Wyman W. "Henry Stevens sweeps the states." **Papers of the Bibliographical Society of America,** 52 (Fourth quarter, 1958), 249-61.

Pickering, Ernest. **The homes of America.** New York: Thomas Y. Crowell, 1951.

Pratt, Richard. **A treasury of early American homes** New York: Whittlesey House, 1949.

Prussing, Eugene E. **The estate of George Washington, deceased.** Boston: Little, Brown and Company, 1927.

Reif, Rita. **Treasure rooms of America's mansions, manors, and houses.** New York: Coward-McCann, Inc., 1970.

Ross, Ishbel. **Taste in America, an illustrated history of the evolution of architecture, furnishings, fashions, and customs of the American people.** New York: Thomas Y. Crowell, 1967.

Sale, Edith Tunis. **Colonial interiors, Southern Colonial and early Federal.** 2nd series. New York: Bonanza Books, 1930.

Schlesinger, Arthur M. **The birth of a nation, a portrait of the American people on the eve of Independence.** New York: Alfred A. Knopf, 1968.

Schroeder-Lossing. **Life and times of Washington.** Albany, New York: M. M. Belcher Publishing Company, 1903.

Smith, James Morton, ed. **George Washington, a profile.** New York: Hill and Wang, 1969.

Sparks, Jared. **The life of George Washington.** New York: A. L. Burt Company, 1902.

Tallmadge, Thomas E. **The story of architecture in America.** New York: W. W. Norton & Company, Inc., 1936.

Thane, Elswyth. **Mount Vernon, the legacy.** Philadelphia: Lippincott, 1967.

Towner, Harriet C. **The Mount Vernon library.** Mount Vernon, Virginia: Mount Vernon Ladies' Association of the Union, 1937.

Trevelyan, G. M. **Illustrated English social history.** 4 vols. New York: David McKay, 1965.

Tunis, Edwin. **Colonial craftsmen and the beginnings of American industry.** Cleveland: World Publishing Company, 1965.

Tunis, Edwin. **Colonial living.** Cleveland: World Publishing Company, 1957.

Tunis, Edwin. **Shaw's fortune, the picture story of a colonial plantation.** Cleveland: World Publishing Company, 1966.

United States George Washington Bicentennial Commission. **History of the George Washington Bicentennial Celebration.** 3 vols. Washington, D.C.: United States George Washington Bicentennial Commission, 1932.

Vaughn, Alden T. **America before the Revolution, 1725-1775.** Englewood Cliffs, New Jersey: Prentice-Hall, 1967.

Wall, Charles C. "Notes on the early history of Mount Vernon." **William and Mary Quarterly,** II, No. 2, Third Series (April, 1945), 173-90.

Watson, Winslow C., ed. **Men & times of the Revolution, or memoirs of Elkanah Watson.** New York: Dana & Co., 1857.

Wertenbaker, Thomas Jefferson. **The first Americans, 1607-1690.** Vol. II of **History of American life series.** New York: Macmillan Company, 1929.

Williams, Henry Lionel and Williams, Ottalie. **America's small houses.** New York: Bonanza Books, 1964.

Williams, Henry Lionel and Williams, Ottalie. **A guide to old American houses.** New York: A. S. Barnes and Company, Inc., 1962.

Williams, Morley Jeffers, "Washington's changes at Mount Vernon plantation." **Landscape Architecture,** XXVII, No. 2 (January, 1938), p. 69.

Wilstach, Paul. **Mount Vernon, Washington's home and the nation's shrine.** Garden City, New York: Doubleday, Page & Company, 1916.

Wilstach, Paul. **Tidewater Maryland.** Indianapolis: Bobbs-Merrill Company, 1931.

Wish, Harvey. **Society and thought in early America,** Vol. I. New York: Longman, Green, 1953.

Woodward, W. E. **George Washington, the image and the man.** New York: Blue Ribbon Books, 1926.

Wright, Louis B. **The Atlantic frontier, colonial American civilization, 1607-1763.** Ithaca, New York: Cornell University Press, 1965.

Wright, Louis B. **The cultural life of the American colonies, 1607-1763.** New York: Harper & Brothers, 1957.

Index

(For individual titles of books owned by George Washington, see the entry for "Washington, George, library, books, by title" and Appendix II.)

Of this book 2,000 copies have been printed on 70 lb. Warren's Old Style, with the exception of pages 69 to 72, the color section, which is printed on 70 lb. Warren's Lustre Off-Set Enamel. The typesetting for the entire book is Paladium, ranging from 8 to 24 points. The book was printed at The University of Oklahoma Press, Norman, Oklahoma.

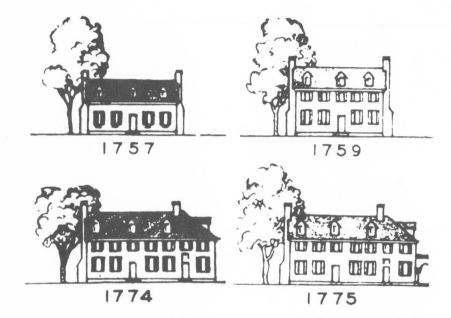

1757   1759

1774   1775